Windows Vista™: A View from the Top

W9-AHK-544

Windows Vista brings a new look to the familiar Windows XP desktop and taskbar, but the Sidebar is the new star. The Sidebar, that long strip along the desktop's right side, lets you mix and match Gadgets — small specialty programs like the headline reader, egg timer, clock, and calculator seen here. In Vista's Aero Glass mode, note how the Start menu and Sidebar are translucent, allowing parts of the desktop to shine through.

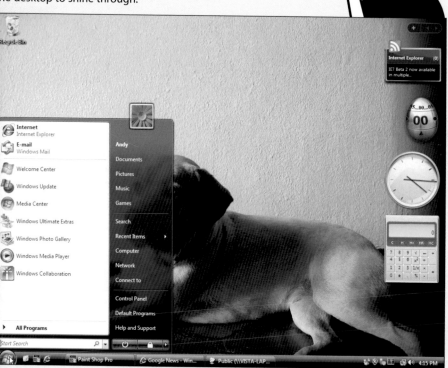

With the new Aero Glass look, the corner button glows when your mouse pointer rests above it (left). Rest your mouse pointer above any button on the taskbar, and Aero Glass shows a thumbnail view of the window (right).

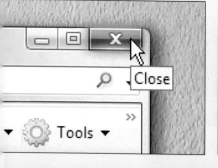

Vista's Aero Basic Look

If your PC isn't powerful enough to run Vista's Aero Glass mode (shown on the preceding page), Vista slips into Aero Basic mode, shown here. Note how the Start menu is no longer translucent: You can't see the desktop (or the dog's face) behind it.

In Aero Basic mode, the corner button no longer glows (left). And instead of showing thumbnail views of taskbar windows, Vista displays only the name (right).

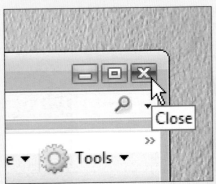

Finding Vista's Windows

PCs with graphics powerful enough for Aero Glass mode let you cycle through open windows in this view. Hold down your Windows key and press Tab to move from one window to another; let go of Tab when your lost window cycles to the front.

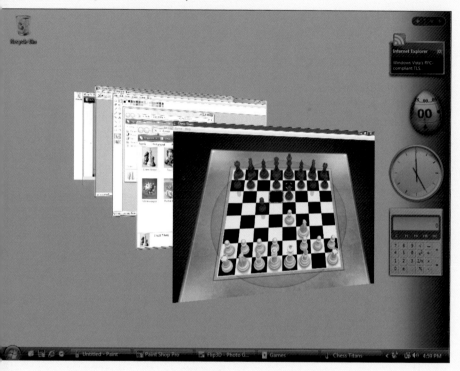

PCs running Aero Basic can display open windows only this way, much like what you already see in Windows XP.

Vista's Documents Folder

The Preview pane along the bottom shows you details about the file you select. Each window's menu bar along the top changes its assortment of buttons as your view changes. The buttons let you know exactly what you can do with the items inside that particular window.

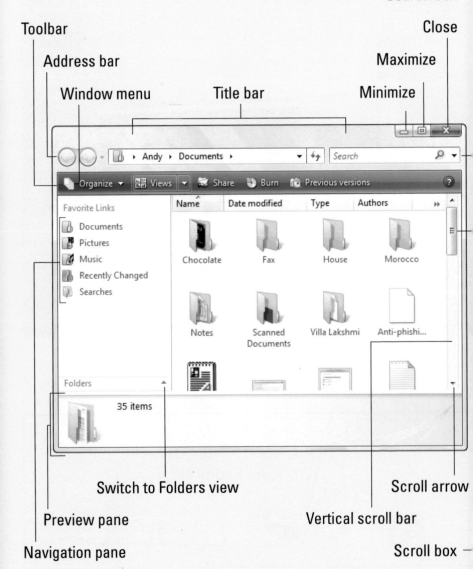

Search box

Close

Maximize

Minimize

Toolbar

Address bar

Window menu

Title bar

Switch to Folders view

Scroll arrow

Preview pane

Vertical scroll bar

Navigation pane

Scroll box

Finding Your Way Around in Windows

Vista offers several ways to move through folders. The top of the Navigation pane lets you move quickly to favorite areas. The Navigation pane's bottom half offers a traditional "branching tree" view of folders, much like the Explorer view in Windows XP.

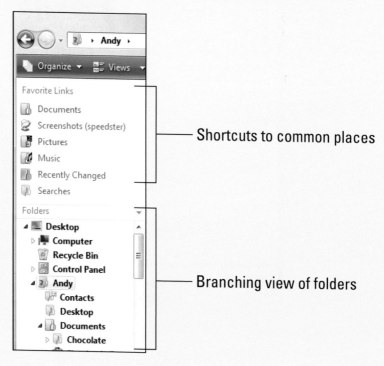

Shortcuts to common places

Branching view of folders

The Address bar at the top of every folder also lets you jump from one folder to another. Click the little arrow next to the word Documents, for example, and a menu lets you jump quickly to any folder within the Documents folder.

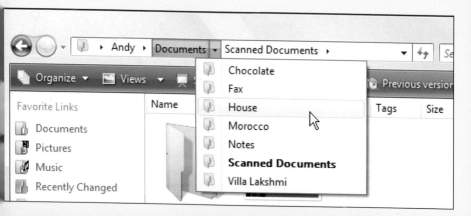

Finding Information

Vista creates an index of every file you create. The handy Search box on the Start menu uses the index to help you find files quickly and easily.

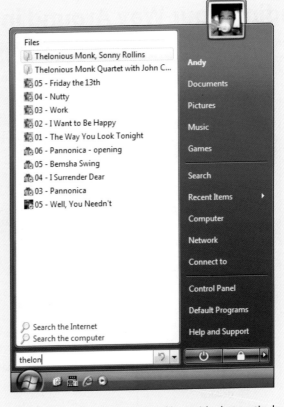

A Search box at the top of every folder lets you quickly locate files inside that particular folder.

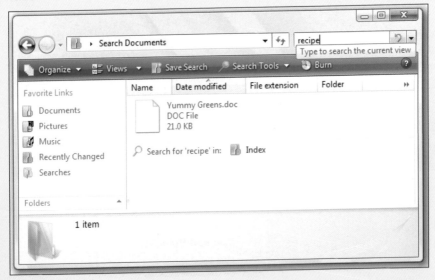

Exploring the Internet

Internet Explorer now lets you keep several Web pages open simultaneously. Clicking the tabs along the top lets you move among the open pages.

Internet Explorer offers a preview of each open page, letting you easily spot and click on the page you want to view.

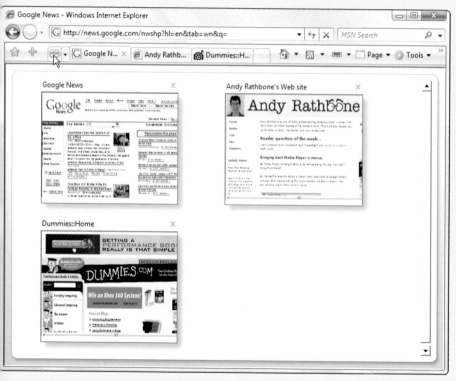

Parental Controls

Vista also creates a detailed log of your children's computer usage, letting you know exactly when they accessed certain Web sites and programs. Vista reminds you each week to read the log and presents you with a quick, one-page synopsis of your children's activities. With Parental Controls, you can keep your kids away from the PC during certain hours, stop them from installing programs, and designate certain programs and Web sites as off limits.

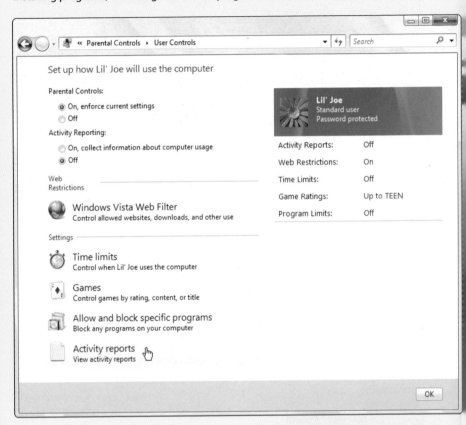

Windows Vista™

FOR

DUMMIES®

SPECIAL PREVIEW EDITION

Text and screen shots are based
on the Beta 2 release of Windows
Vista and Office 2007.

Windows Vista™

FOR

DUMMIES®

SPECIAL PREVIEW EDITION

by Andy Rathbone

WILEY

Wiley Publishing, Inc.

Windows Vista™ For Dummies®, Special Preview Edition

Published by
Wiley Publishing, Inc.
111 River Street
Hoboken, NJ 07030-5774
www.wiley.com

WILEY

About the Author

Andy Rathbone started geeking around with computers in 1985 when he bought a 26-pound portable CP/M Kaypro 2X. Like other nerds of the day, he soon began plying with null-modem adapters, dialing computer bulletin boards, and working part-time at Radio Shack.

He wrote articles for various techie publications before moving to computer books in 1992. He's written the *Windows For Dummies* series, *Upgrading & Fixing PCs For Dummies*, *TiVo For Dummies*, *PCs: The Missing Manual*, and many other computer books.

Today, he has more than 15 million copies of his books in print, and they've been translated into more than 30 languages. Andy can be reached at his Web site, www.andyrathbone.com.

Dedication

To my father, who built his own Heathkit O-11 5" Extra Duty Oscilloscope in the garage.

Author's Acknowledgments

Special thanks to Dan Gookin, Matt Wagner, Tina Rathbone, Steve Hayes, Kelly Ewing, Colleen Totz, Dave Diamond, Joyce Nielsen, Jodi Jensen, Amanda Foxworth, and Ryan Steffen. Thanks also to all the folks I never meet in editorial, sales, marketing, proofreading, layout, graphics, and manufacturing who work hard to bring you this book.

Publisher's Acknowledgments

We're proud of this book; please send us your comments through our online registration form located at www.dummies.com/register/.

Some of the people who helped bring this book to market include the following:

Acquisitions, Editorial, and Media Development

Project Editor: Kelly Ewing

Senior Acquisitions Editor: Steve Hayes

Technical Editor: Joyce Nielsen

Editorial Manager: Jodi Jensen

Media Development Manager: Laura VanWinkle

Editorial Assistant: Amanda Foxworth

Sr. Editorial Assistant: Cherie Case

Cartoons: Rich Tennant (www.the5thwave.com)

Composition Services

Project Coordinator: Ryan Steffen

Layout and Graphics: Carl Byers, Andrea Dahl, Barbara Moore

Proofreaders: Debbye Butler, Amanda Foxworth, Leeann Harney, Dwight Ramsey

Indexer: Techbooks

Publishing and Editorial for Technology Dummies

Richard Swadley, Vice President and Executive Group Publisher

Andy Cummings, Vice President and Publisher

Mary Bednarek, Executive Acquisitions Director

Mary C. Corder, Editorial Director

Publishing for Consumer Dummies

Diane Graves Steele, Vice President and Publisher

Joyce Pepple, Acquisitions Director

Composition Services

Gerry Fahey, Vice President of Production Services

Debbie Stailey, Director of Composition Services

Contents at a Glance

Table of Contents

Introduction

● ●

*W*elcome to the preview for *Windows Vista For Dummies.* This book introduces you to Microsoft's latest version of Windows, *Windows Vista.* This preview book isn't meant to replace *Windows Vista For Dummies.* Microsoft hasn't even finished creating Vista yet. This book, rather, helps you know what Vista does, whether your PC is powerful enough to run it, and whether Vista's worth an upgrade.

If you're brave enough to download a "preview" version of Vista from Microsoft (`www.microsoft.com/windowsvista`), this book offers enough information to keep you on your feet.

About This Book

Microsoft has packed dozens of new features into Vista, giving Windows an agonizingly thorough security lock-down. They've made the window frames translucent, so your desktop shines eerily from below. Microsoft's rearranged Windows XP's trusty menus, and even removed some. Yet, with all these changes, Microsoft's hoping that Vista won't frighten away potential users.

This book explains the following things about Vista:

- ✔ Understanding which of Vista's five versions you need
- ✔ Knowing whether your PC's powerful enough to run Vista
- ✔ Understanding (and turning off) Vista's omnipresent security screens
- ✔ Quickly finding the file you saved or downloaded yesterday
- ✔ Restricting what your kids can do on the PC
- ✔ Copying information to and from a CD or DVD

✔ Printing and scanning your work

✔ Fixing Windows Vista when it's misbehaving

Like all *For Dummies* books, this preview makes it easy to find your information. Just turn to the page you need and read the brief explanation.

How to Use This Book

When something in Windows Vista has you stumped, look for the troublesome topic in this book's table of contents or index. The table of contents lists the chapter names, section titles, and page numbers. The index lists alphabetized topics and page numbers.

Once you've located the spot that deals with that particular bit of computer wizardry, read only what you want to.

If you're feeling spunky and want to learn something, read a little further. You can find a few completely voluntary extra details or some helpful cross-references to check out.

If you have to type something into the computer, you'll see easy-to-follow bold text like this:

Type **Media Player** in the Search box.

That means to type the words *Media Player* and then press the keyboard's Enter key. Typing words into a computer can be confusing, so a description of what you're supposed to type usually follows.

Whenever I describe a Web address or cryptic message you see on the screen, I present it this way:

www.andyrathbone.com

In addition, if you see something like File⇨Open, don't panic. I'm simply giving you a series of commands — in this, choose the File menu and then choose Open.

Finally, keep in mind that this book is a preview. Some figures may change slightly from the version of Vista appearing in early 2007. Microsoft may tweak a sentence or two in the menus, and some minor features may be dropped. But this preview still gives you a good heads up on what to expect when you experience Vista — and you will, probably sooner than you think.

How This Book Is Organized

This preview book contains three parts, each divided into chapters relating to the part's theme. I divided each chapter into short sections to help you figure out Vista's new setup. Sometimes, you may find what you're looking for in a small, boxed sidebar. Other times, you may need to cruise through an entire section or chapter. It's up to you and the particular task at hand.

Here's what awaits you inside.

Part 1: Windows Vista Stuff Everybody Thinks You Already Know

This part dissects Windows Vista's backbone: Its ever-present Welcome Center screen, the reshuffled Start button menu, and your computer's desktop — the work area where all your programs live. It also sheds light on why Vista looks so different when running on different PCs.

It explains how to move windows around Vista's new desktop, as well as Vista's new flashy trick for letting you fetch a window that's somehow disappeared.

Part II: Working with Programs and Files

Here's where you see the underlying mechanics of Windows Vista: How it starts programs, finds the right files, and lets you move information between them all. If an important file or program has vanished from the radar, you discover how to make Windows Vista search your computer's crowded cupboards and bring it back.

Part III: The Part of Tens

Some tidbits of knowledge just can't be categorized very easily. When a piece of information doesn't fall neatly into one of this book's chapters or sections, I toss it in here, the Part of Tens section. Here, you find ten reasons why you should upgrade to Vista and ten new ways of doing old things in Microsoft Office 2007. In addition, I give you ten ways to keep your computer running well.

Icons Used in This Book

Windows Vista is loaded with *icons,* which are little push-button pictures for starting various programs. The icons in this book fit right in. They're even a little easier to figure out:

This signpost warns you that complex, explanatory technical information is coming around the bend. Swerve away from this icon to stay safe from awful technical drivel, unless you happen to be curious about the dry, bare-knuckle mechanics of Vista.

This icon alerts you about juicy information that makes computing easier: A tried-and-true method for keeping the cat off the top of the monitor, for example.

Don't forget to remember these important points. (Or at least dog-ear the pages so that you can return a few days later.)

The computer won't explode while you're performing the delicate operations associated with this icon. Still, wearing a hardhat and proceeding with caution is a good idea.

Windows XP veterans warily eying Vista should read this section. It explains when a Windows XP feature has been either removed or changed substantially.

Where to Go from Here

Give the pages a quick flip and scan a section or two, getting a taste of Microsoft's new operating system. Please remember, this is *your* book — your weapon against the programmers who've inflicted all these changes upon you. Please circle any paragraphs you find useful, highlight key concepts, add your own sticky notes, and doodle in the margins next to the complicated stuff.

The more you mark up your book, the easier it will be for you to find all the good stuff again.

Part I

Windows Vista Stuff Everybody Thinks You Already Know

The 5th Wave   By Rich Tennant

"Well, the first level of Windows Vista security seems good—I can't get the shrink-wrapping off."

In this part . . .

Most people are dragged into Windows Vista without a choice. Their new computers probably came with Windows Vista already installed. Or maybe the office switched to Windows Vista, where everyone has to learn it except for the boss, who doesn't have a computer. Or maybe Microsoft's marketing hype pushed you into it.

Whatever your situation, this part gives you a refresher on Windows Vista basics and buzzwords such as dragging and dropping, cutting and pasting, and tugging at vanishing toolbars.

It explains how Vista is changing Windows for the better, and it warns you when Vista has messed things up completely.

Chapter 1

What Is Windows Vista?

*C*hances are, you've probably heard about Windows: the boxes and windows and mouse pointer that greet you whenever you turn on your computer. In fact, millions of people all over the world are puzzling over it as you read this book. Almost every new computer sold today comes with a copy of Windows preinstalled — cheerfully greeting you when first turned on.

This chapter helps you understand why Windows lives inside your computer and introduces Microsoft's latest Windows version, called *Windows Vista.*

What Is Windows Vista, and Why Are You Using It?

Created and sold by a company called Microsoft, Windows isn't like your usual software that lets you write term papers or send angry e-mails to mail-order companies. No, Windows is an *operating system,* meaning it controls the way you work with your computer. It's been around for more than 20 years, and the latest whiz-bang version is called *Windows Vista.*

Windows gets its name from all the cute little windows it places on your monitor. Each window shows information, such as a picture, a program that you're running, or a baffling technical reprimand. You can put several windows on-screen at the same time and jump from window to window, visiting different programs. You can also enlarge a window to fill the entire screen. (Hint: Double-click any window's topmost strip to fill the screen.)

Like the teacher with the whistle on the playground, Windows controls every window on your screen and each part of your computer. When you turn on your computer, Windows jumps onto the screen and supervises any running programs. Throughout all this action, Windows keeps things running smoothly, even if the programs start shoving each other around.

In addition to controlling your computer and bossing around your programs, Windows Vista comes with a bunch of free programs. Although your computer can run without these programs, they're nice to have. These programs let you do different things, like write and print letters, browse the Internet, play music, and even whittle down your camcorder's vacation footage into a three-minute short — automatically.

And why are you using Windows Vista? If you're like most people, you didn't have much choice. A few people escaped Windows by buying Apple computers (those nice-looking computers that cost more). But chances are, you, your neighbors, your boss, your kids at school, and millions of other people around the world are using Windows.

Windows Vista promises to keep its stranglehold on PCs for the following reasons:

✔ Microsoft took pains (and several years of work) to make Windows Vista the most secure version of Windows yet. (Just ask people who upgraded from previous versions.)

✔ Windows makes it easy for several people to share a single computer. Each person receives his or her own user account. When users click their names on the Windows opening screen, they see their *own* work — just the way they left it. Vista adds new controls to allow parents to limit what activities their kids use the PC for, as well as how much of the Internet they can view.

✔ A new, automated version of Backup makes it easier to do what you should have been doing all along: Make copies of your important files every night.

✔ Finally, Vista's powerful new Search box feature means that it's not a disaster if you forget about where you stored your files. Just click the Start menu and type what that file contains in the Start menu's Search box: a few words in a document, the name of the band singing the song, or even the date you took that picture of Kelly at the office party.

Windows Vista: What's Neat and New

Microsoft releases a new version of Windows every few years. If you bought your PC between 2001 and 2005, you've probably grown accustomed to the frightening mechanics of Windows XP. That begs the nagging question, why bother upgrading to Windows Vista when Windows XP works just fine?

Actually, if Windows XP's running just fine, then you probably won't need Windows Vista. But Microsoft hopes the following improvements in Vista will push your hand toward your credit card.

Streamlined Start menu

The bright-blue Start button lives in the bottom-left corner of the desktop, where it's always ready for action. By clicking the Start button, you can start programs, adjust Windows Vista's settings, find help for sticky situations, or, thankfully, shut down Windows Vista and get away from the computer for a while.

Click the Start button once, and the first layer of menus appears, as shown in Figure 1-1.

Figure 1-1: The Start button in Windows Vista hides dozens of menus for starting programs and applications.

Your Start menu will change as you work, constantly updating itself to list your favorite programs on its front page. That's why the Start menu on your friend's computer is probably arranged differently than the Start menu on your computer. Here are a few things to remember about this menu:

✔ Your Documents, Pictures, and Music folders are always one click away on the Start menu. These folders are specially designed for their contents. The Pictures folder, for example, displays little thumbnails of your digital photos. The biggest perk to these three folders? Keeping your files in these logically named folders helps you remember where you stored them.

✔ Vista drops the "My" from the front of your Documents, Pictures and Music folders. But they're the same thing: Places for you to store your files.

✔ Windows thoughtfully places your most frequently used programs along the left side of the Start menu for easy point 'n' click action.

✔ See the words All Programs near the Start menu's bottom left? Click there, and yet another menu opens to offer more options. (That new menu covers up the first, though; to bring back the first menu, simply click the word Back.)

✔ Spot something confusing on the Start menu? Hover your mouse pointer over the mysterious icon. Windows responds with a helpful explanatory message.

✔ Strangely enough, you also click the Start button when you want to *stop* using Windows. (You click either the Power button or Lock button along the Start menu's bottom right.)

Quick search

Instead of forcing you to search for your files time and again, Vista automatically remembers your files' locations. For example, search for every document mentioning "celery," and Vista lets you save the results as a Celery folder. Whenever you create new documents mentioning "celery," Vista automatically drops them into the Celery folder for easy retrieval.

Giving Vista a test run

Microsoft let software developers and other techies download Vista on May 23, 2006, and the general public can download it from Microsoft's Web site (www.microsoft.com/windowsvista). Although giving Vista a sneak peek may sound fun, Vista's quite a demanding piece of software. Here's what you need to run Vista on your PC:

Broadband Internet Connection. You must download a gargantuan 3GB file. That rules out dial-up connections.

DVD burner and software. Vista won't fit onto a CD. Your PC needs both a DVD burner and DVD burning software. (That software must know how to handle an *ISO* file — a way of squeezing a DVD's contents into one file.)

An empty partition. Vista requires a special spot on your PC's hard drive known as a *partition*. If you're like most people, Windows XP already lives on your hard drive's only partition. That means you must either delete Windows XP and all your files or install Vista on a second hard drive.

If you can't help yourself, download Vista at Microsoft's Web site. Although the download's no charge, don't think you're upgrading your PC for free: Vista still squirms with bugs, and Microsoft built-in a kill-switch that kicks in after several months.

Live taskbar thumbnails and other visual cues

Try this

Microsoft spent some time decorating Vista with a three-dimensional look. When you can't find an open window, for example, hold down the Windows key and press Tab. All the open windows appear on your PC in a Flip 3D view, shown in Figure 1-2.

Figure 1-2: Press the Windows key and Tab to see a 3D-view of your currently open windows.

Hover your mouse pointer over any name listed on your desktop's taskbar, and Vista displays a thumbnail picture of that window's current contents, making the window you're looking for much easier to retrieve from the sea of programs.

Integrated multimedia experience

Vista's new version of Media Player sports streamlined, easier-to-use controls. The big star, however, is Vista's Media Center, which lets you watch television on your PC and even record shows onto your hard drive for later viewing.

Recording TV shows requires two important things, however: a TV tuner in your PC and the proper version of Vista. (Vista comes in a startling *five* versions.) Installing a TV tuner can be as simple as plugging a box into your PC's USB port or sliding a card inside your PC.

The Five Flavors of Vista

Windows XP came in two easy-to-understand versions: One for home, and one for businesses. Microsoft confuses things in Vista by splitting it into five different versions, each with a different price tag.

Luckily, only three versions are aimed at consumers, and most people will probably choose Windows Vista Home Premium. Still, to clear up the confusion, I describe all five versions in Table 1-1.

Table 1-1	The Five Flavors of Windows Vista
The Version of Vista	**What It Does**
Windows Vista Home Basic	Reminiscent of Windows XP Home Edition, this version leaves out Vista's fancier media features, such as DVD-movie burning, HDTV, TV recording, and other similar features. (You can still burn files to a DVD, though.) The backup program isn't automated, unfortunately, so you need to remember to back up your files.
	As a final blow, Microsoft left out Vista's Aero "glass" look shown in this book's color preview pages — Aero glass won't appear even if your PC's video is souped-up enough to handle the graphics.
Windows Vista Home Premium	This version is Windows Vista Home Basic, but with the media features and the Aero glass look tossed back in. It targets people who watch TV on their PC or want to create DVDs from their camcorder footage. Plus, the backup program is automated, taking place whenever you want.

(continued)

Table 1-1 *(continued)*

The Version of Vista	What It Does
Windows Vista Business	Just as with its brethren, Windows XP Professional, this aims at the business market. It includes the built-in fax program, for instance, something not found in either home version.
Windows Vista Enterprise	This business market version contains even more tools, such as support for advanced computer setups.
Windows Vista Ultimate	This version contains everything found in the Vista Home Premium and Vista Business versions. It's aimed at the wallets of hard-core PC users, such as gamers, people in the video industry, and similar people who spend their lives in front of their keyboards.

Although five versions may seem complicated, choosing the one you need isn't that difficult. And because Microsoft stuffed all the versions on your Vista DVD, you can upgrade at any time simply by whipping out the credit card, visiting an online site, and downloading software that unlocks the features in a different version.

Which one's for you? Run through the following list to see what features are most important to you:

- ✔ If your PC can't display or record TV shows, and you don't want to make DVDs from your camcorder footage, then save a few bucks by sticking with **Windows Vista Home Basic.** It's fine for word processing, e-mail, and the Internet.

- ✔ If you want to burn DVDs and/or record TV shows on your PC, then pony up the cash for **Windows Vista Home Premium.**

- ✔ People who run Web servers on their PC — and you'll know if you're doing it — will want **Windows Vista Business.**

✔ Dedicated gamers with hot-rod PCs will want **Windows Vista Ultimate** for its extra gaming tweaks. Plus, it has *everything* in the previous versions — there's no chance of missing a feature you spot on somebody else's PC.

✔ Computer techies who work for businesses will argue with their boss over whether they need **Windows Business** or **Windows Enterprise** versions.

That inexpensive **Vista Starter** version you may have heard about isn't sold in the United States. It's sold at reduced prices in developing nations like Malaysia. (It's not really a goodwill gesture as much as it's an attempt to reduce software piracy.)

Chapter 2

The Desktop, Sidebar, and Other Windows Vista Goodies

. . . .

In This Chapter

▶ Starting Windows Vista

▶ Using the desktop and other Windows Vista features

▶ Reading the taskbar

▶ Introducing the Sidebar

. . . .

*T*his chapter provides a drive-by tour of Windows Vista. You turn on your computer, start Windows, and spend a few minutes gawking at Vista's various neighborhoods, including the desktop, taskbar, and Sidebar.

The programs you're using hang out on the Windows *desktop* (a fancy word for the Windows background). The taskbar serves as a head turner, letting you move easily from one program to another.

Starting and Stopping in Windows Vista

Starting Windows Vista is as easy as turning on your computer — Vista leaps onto the screen automatically with a futuristic flourish.

Click the Start button, and the Start menu pops up from the button's head. If you see an icon for your desired program, click it, and Windows loads the program.

Strangely enough, you also click the Start button when you want to *stop* using Windows. If the Start menu is hiding, hold down Ctrl and press Esc to bring it back from behind the trees. Then, to stop using Windows, you want one of the two buttons resting at the bottom of the Start menu:

✔ **Sleep:** Sleep mode comes in handy when you won't be using your PC for several hours but will want to start up exactly where you left off. Designed for on-the-go laptoppers and impatient desktoppers, this option saves your work and then puts your PC in a low-power state. But when you open your laptop's lid or turn on your PC, your open programs and documents are right where you left them on the desktop.

✔ **Lock:** Meant for short trips to the water cooler, this option simply locks access to your desktop, and places your User Account picture on the screen. When you return, type your password, and Vista instantly displays your desktop again, just as you left it.

Windows Vista offers several other ways to close your session. Look closely at the arrow to the right of the Lock button. Click the arrow to see additional action options, shown in Figure 2-1:

✔ **Switch User:** If somebody else just wants to borrow the computer for a few minutes, choose Switch User. The Welcome screen appears, but Windows keeps your open programs waiting in the background. When you switch back, everything's just as you left it. (Personally, I think Log Off makes more sense.)

✔ **Log Off:** Choose this option when you're through working at the PC and somebody else wants a go at it. Windows saves your work and your settings and returns to the log on screen, ready for the next user.

✔ **Lock:** In case you missed the Lock button itself, Microsoft offers the Lock option again.

✔ **Restart:** Only choose this option when Windows Vista acts up — several programs crashed, or Windows seems to be acting awfully weird. Windows Vista turns off and reloads itself, hopefully feeling refreshed.

✔ **Sleep:** Microsoft also offers the Sleep option here.

✔ **Hibernate:** Usually found on laptops, this option saves your session and then turns off the computer. Use this option when you will be away from your computer for a considerable period of time (several hours or overnight), but want to return to the current work session.

✔ **Shut Down:** Choose this option when nobody else will be using the computer until at least the next morning. Windows Vista saves all files and settings and turns off your computer.

Figure 2-1: Click the little arrow to see more options for wrapping up work on your PC.

When you tell Windows Vista that you want to quit, it searches through all your open windows to see whether you've saved all your work. If it finds any work you've forgotten to save, it prompts you so that you can save it before exiting. Whew!

This could be the answer °°

You don't *have* to shut down Windows Vista. In fact, some people leave their computers turned on all the time, saying it's better for their computer's health. Others say that their computers are healthier if they're turned off each day. However, *everybody* says to turn off your monitor when you're done working. Monitors definitely enjoy cooling down when not in use.

Don't just press your PC's Off button to turn off your PC. Instead, be sure to shut down Windows Vista through one of its official Off options. Otherwise, Windows Vista can't properly prepare your computer for the dramatic event and may nag you about an "improper shutdown" upon your return.

Organizing Your Desktop

Normally, people want their desktops to be horizontal, not vertical. Keeping pencils from rolling off a normal desk is hard enough. But in Windows Vista, your monitor's screen is known as the Windows *desktop,* and that's where all your work takes place. You can create files and folders to reside on your new electronic desktop and arrange them all across the screen. Each program runs in its own little *window* on top of the desktop.

Windows Vista starts with a freshly scrubbed, nearly empty desktop. After you've been working for a while, your desktop will fill up with *icons* — little graphic push buttons that load your files with a quick double-click of the mouse. Some people leave their desktops strewn with icons for easy access. Others organize their work: When they finish working on something, they store it in a *folder.*

The desktop boasts these four main parts, shown in Figure 2-2:

✔ **Taskbar:** Resting lazily along the desktop's bottom edge, the taskbar lists the programs and files you're currently working on. (Point at any program's name on the taskbar to see a thumbnail photo of that program, as shown in Figure 2-2.)

✔ **Start menu:** Seen at the taskbar's left edge, the Start menu works like the restaurant's waiter: It presents menus at your bidding, letting you choose what program to run or file to open.

✔ **Sidebar:** When Windows Vista first starts, you see the *Sidebar,* that strip along the right edge that can also be hidden if you so choose. However, you may become hooked on its plethora of customized gadgets, such as weather forecasters, search boxes, and Sudoku games.

✔ **Recycle Bin:** The desktop's *Recycle Bin,* that little wastebasket-shaped icon, stores your recently deleted files for easy retrieval. Whew!

Here's some other stuff to keep in mind while working with the desktop:

Figure 2-2: The Windows Vista desktop, which spreads across your entire computer screen, has four main parts: The Start button, taskbar, Recycle Bin, and the optional Sidebar.

I'm smart —

✔ You can start new projects (such as a new worksheet, presentation, or journal entry) directly from your desktop: Right-click the desktop, choose New, and select the project of your dreams from the pop-up menu. (The menu lists most of your computer's programs for quick 'n' easy access.)

✔ Are you befuddled about some object's reason for being? Timidly rest the pointer over the mysterious doodad, and Windows will pop up a little box explaining what that thing is or does. Right-click on the object, and ever helpful Windows Vista usually tosses up a menu listing nearly everything you can do with that particular object. This trick works on most icons found on your desktop and throughout your programs.

✔ All the icons on your desktop may suddenly disappear, leaving it completely empty. Chances are, Windows Vista hid them in a misguided attempt to be helpful. To bring your work back to life, right-click on your empty desktop and choose View from the pop-up menu. Finally, ensure that the Show Desktop Icons entry is checked, which makes everything reappear with no harm done.

Finding Visual Cues on the Taskbar

This section introduces one of Windows Vista's handiest tricks, so pull in your chair a little closer. Whenever you run more than one window on the desktop, there's a big problem: Programs and windows tend to cover up each other, making them difficult to locate.

Windows Vista's solution is the *taskbar* — a special area that keeps track of all your open programs. Shown in Figure 2-3, the taskbar normally lives along the bottom of your screen, although you can move it to any edge you want. (*Hint:* Just drag it from edge to edge. If it doesn't move, right-click on the taskbar and click Lock the Taskbar to remove the check mark by its name. Then drag to whichever edge of the screen you desire.)

Figure 2-3: Click buttons for currently running programs on the taskbar.

Rest your mouse pointer over any of the taskbar's programs to see a thumbnail image of that program, shown in Figure 2-3, even if that program is currently covered by other windows on your desktop.

See how the button for Paint Shop Pro looks darker than the other taskbar buttons in Figure 2-3? That's because Paint Shop Pro is currently the *active* window on the desktop: It's the program currently waiting for you to start working. One or more of your taskbar's buttons always look darker unless you close or minimize all the windows on your desktop.

From the taskbar, you can perform powerful magic on your open windows, as described in the following list:

- To play with a program listed on the taskbar, click its name. The window rises to the surface and rests atop any other open windows, ready for action.

- To close a window listed on the taskbar, *right-click* on its name and choose Close from the pop-up menu. The program quits, just as if you'd chosen its Exit command from within its own window. (The departing program first gives you a chance to save your work before it quits and walks off the screen.)

- Don't see the taskbar? If only the taskbar's top edge peeks up along the screen's bottom, grab the visible part with your mouse and drag it upward until the entire taskbar is visible. (Consider right-clicking on the taskbar and choosing Lock the Taskbar to keep it locked in place if it routinely gets moved out of view.)

Shrinking windows to the taskbar and retrieving them

Windows spawn windows. You start with one window to write a letter of praise to the local opera house. You open another window to check an address, for example, and then yet another to see whether you've forgotten any upcoming shows. Before you know it, four more windows are crowded across the desktop.

To combat the clutter, Windows Vista provides a simple means of window control: You can transform a window from a screen-cluttering square into a tiny button on the *taskbar,* which sits along the bottom of the screen. The solution is the Minimize button.

See the three buttons lurking in just about every window's top-right corner? Click the *Minimize button* — the button with the little line in it, as shown in the margin. Whoosh! The window disappears, represented by its little button on the taskbar at your screen's bottom.

Here's some more info on the Minimize button:

- To make a minimized program on the taskbar revert into a regular, on-screen window, just click its name on the taskbar. Pretty simple, huh?

✓ Each taskbar button shows the name of the program it represents. And if you hover your mouse pointer over the taskbar button, Vista displays a thumbnail photo of that program.

✓ When you minimize a window, you neither destroy its contents nor close the program. And when you click the window's name on the taskbar, it reopens to the same size you left it, showing its same contents.

✓ Whenever you load a program, its name automatically appears on the taskbar. If one of your open windows ever gets lost on your desktop, click its name on the taskbar to bring it to the forefront.

Clicking the taskbar's sensitive areas

Like a crafty card player, the taskbar comes with a few tips and tricks. You can see some of them in Figure 2-4. Here's the lowdown on the icons near the taskbar's right edge, known as the *notification area:*

✓ **Clock:** Hold the mouse pointer over the clock, and Windows Vista shows the current day and date. If you want to change the time, date, or even add a second time zone, a double-click on the clock summons the Windows Vista time/date change program.

✓ **Arrows:** Sometimes the taskbar hides things. Click the little arrow on the left (shown in Figure 2-4), and a few hidden icons may slide into view.

✓ **Speaker:** Click the little speaker icon to adjust the sound card's volume. Or double-click the little speaker to bring up a sound-mixing panel.

✓ **Other icons:** These often appear next to the clock, depending on what Windows Vista is up to. If you're printing, for example, a little printer icon appears there. Laptops often show a battery-power-level gauge. As with all the other icons down there, if you double-click the printer or battery gauge, Windows Vista brings up information about the printer's or battery's current status.

TIP

📌 **Blank part:** The empty portions of the taskbar also hide a menu. Want to minimize all your desktop's open windows in a hurry? Right-click on a blank part of the taskbar and choose Show the Desktop from the pop-up menu.

✓ check this out —

Figure 2-4: These taskbar icons help with specific functions.

To organize your open windows, right-click on a blank part of the taskbar and choose one of the Show Windows commands. Windows Vista scoops up all your open windows and lays them back down in neat, orderly squares.

Introducing the Sidebar

People who can afford enormous monitors love Vista's new Sidebar, that gadget-packed strip along the desktop's right edge. People with small monitors may find it a bothersome waste of space.

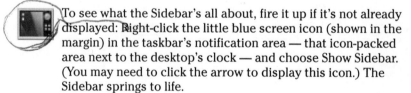

To see what the Sidebar's all about, fire it up if it's not already displayed: Right-click the little blue screen icon (shown in the margin) in the taskbar's notification area — that icon-packed area next to the desktop's clock — and choose Show Sidebar. (You may need to click the arrow to display this icon.) The Sidebar springs to life.

To see Windows Vista's collection of built-in *Gadgets* (minuscule programs that snap on and off their panel), click the little plus sign near the Sidebar's top edge. A window pops up offering a clock and slideshow, among others. Click Get More Gadgets Online to head to Gadget nirvana: A Web site packed with Gadgets, ready for the picking.

Looks Like Fun

    ✓ Prefer your Sudoku game gadget on top? Drag it up there.
      You can even drag Gadgets off the Sidebar and onto the
      desktop — if you have a huge enough monitor to sacri-
      fice the space.

    ✓ To change a Gadget's settings — such as to choose which
      photos appear in your Slideshow, for example — point at
      the Gadget and click the little checkmark that appears.
      To remove a Gadget completely, click the little X instead.

Chapter 3

Getting Around in Windows and Folders

*T*his chapter is for curious Windows anatomy students. You know who you are — you're the ones who see all those buttons, borders, and balloons scattered throughout Windows Vista and wonder what would happen if you just clicked that little thing over there.

This rather gruesome chapter tosses an ordinary window (your oft-used Documents folder, to be precise) onto the dissection table. I've yanked out each part for labeling and explanation.

A standard field guide follows, identifying and explaining the buttons, boxes, windows, bars, lists, and other oddities you may encounter when you're trying to make Windows Vista do something useful.

Feel free to don any protective gear you may have lying about, use the margins to scribble notes, and tread forcefully into the world of Windows.

Dissecting a Typical Window

Figure 3-1 places a typical window on the slab, with all its parts labeled. You might recognize the window as your Documents folder, that storage tank for most of your work.

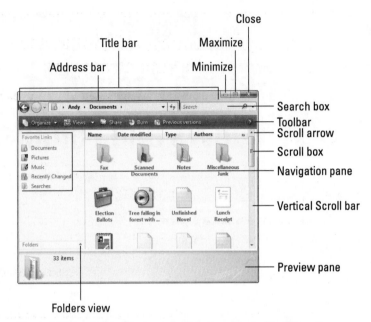

Figure 3-1: Here's how the ever-precise computer nerds address the different parts of a window.

Just as boxers grimace differently depending on where they've been punched, windows behave differently depending on where they've been clicked. The next few sections describe the main parts of the Documents folder's window in Figure 3-1, how to click them, and how Windows responds.

✔ Windows XP veterans remember their My Documents folder, which stashed all their files. Vista drops the word My to create the Documents folder. (You're still supposed to stash your files inside it.) Other My hatchet jobs include the Pictures and Music folders.

✔ Windows Vista is full of little weird-shaped buttons, borders, and boxes. It's not important to remember all their names, although that would give you a leg up on figuring out Windows' scholarly Help menus. When you spot an odd portion of a window, just return to this chapter, look up its name in Figure 3-1, and read its explanation.

Clicking, double-clicking, and right-clicking strategies

Clicking or double-clicking your mouse will control nearly everything in Windows, yet Microsoft seems befuddled when defining the difference between the two finger actions. Microsoft says to click when *selecting* something, and double-click when *choosing* something. Huh?

You're *selecting* something when you're highlighting it. For example, you click in a box, on a window, or on a filename to *select* it. That click usually *highlights* the item, preparing it for further action.

Choosing something, by contrast, is much more decisive. An authoritative double-click on a file convinces Windows to open it for you immediately.

Microsoft's theoretical hierarchies bore me, so I almost always take the third option and *right-click* things. Right-click nearly anything to see a little menu listing everything it can do. I click the option I want, and Windows does my bidding.

The moral? *When in doubt, right-click.*

> ✔ Most things in Windows can be dealt with by simply clicking, double-clicking, or right-clicking, a decision explained in the nearby sidebar, "Clicking, double-clicking, and right-clicking strategies." (Spoiler: *When in doubt, always right-click.*)

> ✔ After you click a few windows a few times, you realize how easy it is to boss them around. The hard part is finding the right controls for the *first* time, like figuring out the buttons on that new cell phone.

Browsing, Searching, and Otherwise Fooling with Folders

Found atop nearly every window (see Figure 3-2), the title bar usually lists the name of the program and the file it's currently working on. For example, Figure 3-2 shows the title bar from Windows Vista's Notepad program. It lists an unnamed file because you haven't had a chance to save and name the file yet. (It may be full of notes you've jotted down from an energetic phone conversation with Ed McMahon.)

Figure 3-2: A title bar.

Although mild-mannered, the mundane title bar holds hidden powers, described in the following tips:

✔ Title bars make convenient handles for moving windows around your desktop. Point at the title bar, hold down the mouse button, and move the mouse around: The window follows along as you move your mouse. Found the right location? Let go of the mouse button, and the window sets up camp in its new spot.

✔ Double-click the title bar, and the window expands to fill the entire screen. Double-click it again, and the window retreats to its previous size.

✔ In Windows XP, every title bar carried a, well, title of what you were viewing. Vista, however, leaves its folders' names *off* the title bar, preferring an empty strip. Although Vista's title bars may lack titles, they still work like regular title bars: Feel free to drag them around your desktop, just as before.

✔ The window you're currently working with always sports a *highlighted* title bar — it's a different color from the title bars of any other open windows. By glancing at all the title bars on the screen, you can quickly tell which window is awake and accepting anything you type.

✔ The right end of the title bar sports three square buttons. From left to right, they let you minimize, maximize/ restore, or close a window.

Directly beneath every folder's title bar lives the *Address bar*. Internet veterans will experience déjà vu: Vista's Address bar is lifted straight from the top of Internet Explorer and glued atop every folder.

The Address bar's three main parts, described from left to right, perform three different duties:

Back and Forward buttons. These two arrows keep track as you forage through your PC's folders. The Back button back-tracks to the folder you just visited. The Forward button brings you back. (Click the miniscule arrow to the right of the Forward arrow to see a list of places you've visited previously; click any entry to revisit it instantly.)

Address bar. Just as Internet Explorer's Address bar lists a Web site's address, Vista's Address bar displays your current folder's address — its location inside your PC.

Feel free to type a Web site's address — something like www.andyrathbone.com — into any folder's Address bar. Your folder will summon Internet Explorer, which opens to that particular site.

Search box. In another rip-off from Internet Explorer, every Vista folder includes a Search box. Instead of searching the Internet, though, it rummages through your folder's contents. For example, type the word "carrot" into a folder's Search box: Vista digs through the folder's contents and retrieves every file mentioning "carrot."

Dragging, dropping, and running

Although the term *drag and drop* sounds as if it's straight out of a *Sopranos* episode, it's really a nonviolent mouse trick used throughout Windows. Dragging and dropping is a way of moving something — say, an icon on your desktop — from one place to another.

To *drag,* put the mouse pointer over the icon and *hold down* the left or right mouse button. (I prefer the right mouse button.) As you move the mouse across your desk, the pointer drags the icon across the screen. Place the pointer/icon where you want it and release the mouse button. The icon *drops,* unharmed.

Holding down the *right* mouse button while dragging and dropping makes Windows Vista toss up a helpful little menu, asking whether you want to *copy* or *move* the icon.

Helpful Tip Department: Started dragging something and realized midstream that you're dragging the wrong item? Don't let go of the mouse button — instead, press Esc to cancel the action. Whew! (If you've dragged with your right mouse button and already let go of the button, there's another exit: Choose Cancel from the pop-up menu.)

To expand your search beyond that particular folder, click the arrow next to the Search box's magnifying glass icon. A drop-down menu lets you route your search to your entire PC or even the Internet.

When sending a search to the Internet, the Search box normally routes entries off to Microsoft's own Search Provider. (That lets Microsoft get kickbacks from the ads.) To send the search to Google or any other search engine, fire up Internet Explorer and click the little arrow next to the Search box's magnifying glass.

Finding Vista's hidden menu bar

Windows Vista has more menu items than an Asian restaurant. To keep everybody's minds on computer commands instead of seaweed salad, Windows hides its menus inside the *menu bar.*

In fact, Vista even hides every folder's menu bar. To bring them back, press Alt, and they drop into place. To keep them permanently affixed there, choose Folder Options from the Tools menu, click the View tab, and put a checkmark in the box next to Always Show Classic Menus. Click OK.

The menu bar displays a different menu for each word. To reveal the secret options, click any word — *Edit,* for example. A menu tumbles down, as shown in Figure 3-3, presenting options related to editing a file.

Just as restaurants sometimes run out of specials, a window sometimes isn't capable of offering all its menu items. Any unavailable options are *grayed out,* like the menu items above Select All in Figure 3-3. Sometimes options will be grayed out if they simply aren't applicable to what you're currently working on.

If you accidentally click the wrong word, causing the wrong menu to jump down, simply point to the word you *really* wanted on the menu. A forgiving soul, Windows retracts the mistaken menu and displays your newly chosen one.

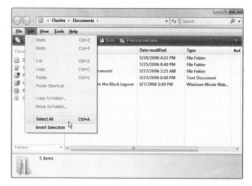

Figure 3-3: Click any word on the menu bar to see its associated menu of commands.

To back out of Menu Land completely, click the mouse pointer back down on your work in the window's *workspace* — the area where you're supposed to be working.

Choosing the right button for the job

Windows XP veterans fondly remember their folders' *Task pane,* a handy strip along a folder's left side that displayed useful buttons for common chores. Once again, Microsoft played the overzealous housekeeper in Vista: The Task pane is reduced to a thin strip of buttons called the *toolbar.*

You don't need to know much about the toolbar, because Vista automatically places the right buttons into the folder that needs them. Open your Music folder, for example, and the toolbar quickly sprouts a Play All button for marathon listening sessions. Open the Pictures folder, and the friendly toolbar serves up a Slide Show button.

If a button's meaning isn't immediately obvious, hover your mouse over it; a little message explains the button's *raison d'être.* My own translations for the most common buttons are in the following bullets:

✔ **Organize:** A click here unveils a menu with several options for managing your folders: Create a new folder, delete a folder, specify folder options, or select everything in the folder, handy when you want to copy or move its contents elsewhere.

The Layout option on the Organize button's menu lets you toggle those thick informational strips along the sides of your window. For example, you can turn the *Navigation pane* — that strip of shortcuts along the left — on or off . You can also turn off the *Preview pane,* that strip along every folder's bottom that displays information about the selected file. **Hint:** If you miss Vista's hidden menu bar, turn it on permanently by clicking the Layout option on the Organize button and choosing Classic Menus.

✔ **Views:** The second button to live atop every folder window, the Views button may be the most useful: It makes the window display your files in different ways. Keep clicking it to cycle through popular icon sizes; stop clicking when one looks good. To jump to a favorite view, click the Views button's adjacent arrow to see a list of every available view. Choose Details, for example, to list everything you ever wanted to know about a file: its size, creation date, and other minutia. (**Hint:** Photos look best when shown in either Large or Extra Large Icons view.)

Are your folder's icons too big or small? Hold down the Ctrl key and roll your mouse's scroll wheel. Roll one direction to enlarge them, the reverse direction to shrink them.

✔ **Share:** Click here to share this folder with somebody on another computer. You won't need this button until you set up a network to link this PC with others.

✔ **Burn:** This button copies your selected items to a temporary folder. Then, when you're ready, you can burn the files from the temporary folder to a disc.

✔ **Help:** Click the little blue question mark icon for help with whatever you happen to be viewing at the time.

Windows Flip (And It Comes in 3D, Too!)

A terrible dealer at the poker table, Windows Vista tosses windows around your desktop in a seemingly random way. Programs cover each other or sometimes dangle off the desktop.

Windows Vista says the window at the top of the pile getting all the attention is called the *active* window. I won't argue. The active window is also the one that receives any keystrokes you or your cat happen to type.

Fortunately, Vista's fancy new 3D view helps you find missing windows. Simply hold down the Windows key and press Tab. Vista does a magician's shuffle with your windows, letting you see them hanging in the air. While holding down the Windows key, keep pressing Tab (or rolling your mouse's scroll wheel) until your lost window has made its way to the front of the pack. Let go of the Windows key to place that window at the top of your desktop. (For more on missing windows, see Chapter 6.)

If your older PC can't handle Vista's 3D View (or if your newer PC's graphics card isn't up to snuff), hold down Alt and press Tab for the two-dimensional substitute that works the same or perhaps better. While holding down Alt, keep pressing Tab until Vista highlights your window; let go of Alt to place your newfound window atop your desktop.

Chapter 4

Personalizing Windows Vista

● ●

In This Chapter

▶ Making Internet, wireless, and hardware connections

▶ Customizing Internet search options

▶ Choosing the programs you want

▶ Assessing your safety with the Security Center

● ●

*I*nside the Control Panel, you see hundreds of switches and options that let you customize Windows' look, feel, and vibe. This chapter explains a few of the switches and sliders you'll want to tweak, primarily those that relate to Internet, hardware, and security settings.

Like driving a car, working with Windows and the Internet is reasonably safe, as long as you steer clear of the wrong neighborhoods and obey traffic signals. This chapter includes a quick primer on safe computing and explains how to avoid viruses, spyware, hijackers, and other Internet parasites.

Making Internet and Wireless Connections

Windows Vista constantly looks for a working Internet connection in your PC. If it finds one, either through a network or wireless hotspot, you're set: Vista passes the news along to Internet Explorer, and your PC can connect to the Internet immediately. But if Vista can't find the Internet — a frequent occurrence with dial-up modems — the job's up to you.

To guide you smoothly through the turmoil of setting up an Internet connection, Vista presents you with a questionnaire, quizzing you about the details. After a bit of interrogation, Vista helps connect your computer to your ISP (Internet Service Provider) so that you can Web surf with the best of them.

 Setting up a network or connecting to a wireless or broadband network? Vista should automatically find the Internet connection and share it with every PC on your network.

 To transfer your existing Internet account settings to or from another computer, use Vista's new Windows Easy Transfer program. Designed for new PC owners, it copies your old PC's files and settings to your new PC.

Your Web browser is your Internet surfboard — your transportation among the Internet's thousands of Web sites. Internet Explorer comes free with Windows Vista, so many people use it out of convenience. Other people prefer browsers published by other software companies, such as Mozilla's Firefox (www.getfirefox.com).

Simply put, you're not forced to stick with Internet Explorer. Feel free to try other browsers, as they all do pretty much the same thing: Take you from one Web site to another.

Adding New Hardware

You don't need to turn off your PC when plugging things like iPods, cameras, or scanners into the USB port. But when you plug something, such as a new video adapter, *inside* your PC, the computer should be turned off. When you turn the computer back on and Windows Vista returns to life, it may or may not notice your surgical handiwork.

Here's the good news, however: If you simply tell Windows Vista to *look* for the new part, it will probably find it. In fact, Windows Vista not only spots the new part but also often recruits a wizard, if needed, to help you set it up. Just open the Control Panel, choose Classic View, and double-click the Add Hardware icon to start the wizard.

If Windows can't locate your newly installed part automatically, you need to contact the part's manufacturer and ask for a Windows Vista *driver* — a piece of software that lets Vista understand the new part. (Drivers are often downloadable from the manufacturer's Web site, available by searching the Internet.) Some drivers come bundled with installation software to minimize installation chores.

Customizing Internet Search Settings

When Vista comes up short while digging for information stored inside your PC, tell it to search the Internet instead. Just as it is nearly impossible to find a book in a library without a card catalog, it is nearly impossible to find a Web site on the Internet without a good index. Luckily, Internet Explorer lets you access an index — known as a *search engine* — through the Search box in its top right corner.

Type a few words into the Search box about what you're seeking — exotic orchids, for example — and press Enter. Internet Explorer fires off your search to MSN, Microsoft's own search engine. If you prefer, you can change that search engine to Google (www.google.com) or any other search engine you like.

In fact, you can add a variety of search engines, routing most of your searches to Google, for example, but sending occasional searches for books and CDs to Amazon. Follow these steps to customize Internet Explorer's Search box to your liking:

1. **Open Internet Explorer and click the downward-pointing arrow on the Search box's right edge.**

   A drop-down menu appears.

2. **Choose Find More Providers.**

   Internet Explorer visits Microsoft's Web site and lists a few dozen popular search engines. Yes, you need to be connected to the Internet to customize Internet Explorer's Search box.

3. **Click your favorite search engine and choose Add Provider from the resulting pop-up window.**

   If you want all your searches to go to one specific search engine — Google, for example — click the Make This My Default Search Provider box. That tells Internet Explorer to automatically send all your searches to that provider.

4. **Feel free to add any other search engines you like as well.**

   Choose other search engines you'd like to add. They'll all appear on the Search box's drop-down menu, shown in Figure 4-1.

Figure 4-1: To route searches to different places, click the arrow to the right of the Search box and choose a search engine to receive the search.

Keep these search-related tips in mind before you hop on the Internet surfboard:

✔ You can change your default search engine at any time by choosing Change Search Defaults from the bottom of the drop-down menu shown in Figure 4-1. A window appears, listing all your search engines; click your favorite and choose Set Default, and Internet Explorer sends it all your searches.

✔ If Google finds Web sites in foreign languages, it often translates them into your own language for you.

 ✔ Sometimes Google brings up a Web site that's been updated and no longer lists what you're searching for. If that happens, click the word *Cached* in Google's description of the site. That brings up a snapshot of the Web site as it looked when it contained what you're searching for.

 ✔ If you click Google's I'm Feeling Lucky button, Google displays the site most likely to contain what you're after. This option works best when searching for common information.

 ✔ Although Google is very handy, it's just one of many ways to find information. The Internet's loaded with other search engines. AltaVista (www.altavista.com) and Yahoo! (www.yahoo.com) are also popular choices.

 ✔ For many years, people have exchanged messages on a section of the Internet called *Usenet*. Divided into thousands of discussion areas, Usenet lets people type in questions about nearly every subject, exchanging information, holding discussions, or simply yelling at each other. It's a fantastic source of computer information from real people, without a corporate filter. To search Usenet in Google, click the word Groups, listed above the search entry box.

 ✔ Searches usually come up with hundreds or even thousands of hits relating to your subject. If you come up with too many, try again and be more specific with each search.

Getting Just the Programs You Want

You don't have to keep programs on your computer if you'll never use them. To uninstall a program:

1. **Call up the Control Panel's Programs icon and choose Installed Programs.**

   Vista lists all the programs installed on your computer, each program's publisher, the date each was installed, and its size.

If your PC's complaining about running out of disk space, uninstall large programs you no longer use. (Click the word Size in the Size column to sort them by size.)

2. **Click the unwanted program's name on the list and click either Remove or Change.**

   The Remove option sweeps the program off your PC. The Change option (if available) enables you to repair a program or add/remove program features.

To install a new program, follow these steps:

1. **Create a restore point *before* installing the new program.**

   The *restore point* creates a snapshot of your computer's most important settings in case the program messes anything up. Name the restore point *Before Installing the Program.* (Be sure to substitute your own program's name.)

2. **Install the program and create a second restore point.**

   After you install the program with the Control Panel's Programs icon, name your new restore point *After Installing the Program.*

   That leaves you two restore points to return to, each with different benefits. If the newly installed program messes things up, return to the first restore point, and Windows forgets the mess. If the new program works fine, then use the *second* restore point when using System Restore in the future. (If you use any older restore points, Windows will forget that you've installed that program.)

Planning for Healthy Computing

Before reading any further, take a minute to check your PC's safety with Windows Vista's Security Center. The Security Center more closely resembles a large panel of On switches than a command post. It lists Windows Vista's four main defenses, tells you whether they're activated, and provides handy On switches to activate any that may be turned off.

Shown in Figure 4-2, the Security Center shows whether you've turned on Windows Firewall, Microsoft's Automatic Updates feature, Malware protection against viruses and spyware, and other security settings like the ones in Internet Explorer and Vista's new User Account Control.

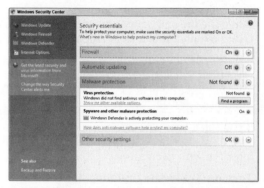

Figure 4-2: The Security Center lets you turn on your computer's main defenses: Windows Firewall, Automatic Updates, and a virus checker.

The computer whose Security Center profile is shown in Figure 4-2 passes the firewall test, as it's listed as On. But the Security Center cautions that Windows isn't updating automatically, nor is it protected from viruses.

All of these defenses should be up and running for maximum safety, because each protects you against different things.

Whenever the Security Center notices that one of Vista's defenses is turned off, it alerts you by placing a red shield icon (shown in the margin) near your taskbar's clock.

To make sure that your computer's big cannons are loaded and pointing in the right direction, open the Security Center and peruse the settings:

1. **Open the Start menu's Control Panel, choose Security, and then choose Security Center.**

   The Security Center leaps into action, shown earlier in Figure 4-2, and displays your computer's current security status. Look for any words that say Off or Not Found and fix the problems, as described in the next four steps.

2. **Turn on the firewall, if necessary.**

Windows Vista's updated, more powerful firewall monitors every connection arriving at your PC's doorstep. When the firewall notices an unrequested connection trying to enter, it blocks it, stopping potential intruders.

If the Security Center lists your firewall as being turned off, click the word Firewall to reveal the Recommendations button and then choose Turn On Windows Firewall.

If you run a firewall from another company, you should turn off Vista's firewall so that the two firewalls don't interfere with each other.

3. **Turn on Automatic Updating, if necessary.**

When turned on, Windows Update automatically checks in with Microsoft through the Internet, downloads any new safety patches and installs them, all for free, without any effort on your part.

If the Security Center doesn't show Automatic Updating as being turned on, click the words Automatic Updating to reveal the Turn On Now button, which you can promptly click to remedy the situation.

4. **Turn on your Malware Protection.**

Vista's Malware protection category contains two separate parts: virus protection and spyware protection.

- **Virus Protection:** Vista doesn't include a built-in virus checker. Nearly every computer and office supply store sells virus-checking software, and you can also buy it online. If Vista can't find a virus-checker on your PC — or it notices that your anti-virus program isn't up-to-date — it warns you here.

- **Spyware and Other Malware Protection:** Vista includes Windows Defender for protecting against spyware. If the Security Center says Windows Defender is turned off, turn it back on by clicking the Recommendations button and choosing Turn On Spyware Scanning for Windows Defender.

5. Turn on your Other Security Settings.

This category covers security settings for both
Internet Explorer and Vista's User Account Control,
otherwise known as "those nagging permission
screens." If the Security Center notices something
astray, here's where you fix the issue:

- **Internet Settings:** Click the Recommendations
  button and choose Restore My Internet Security
  Settings Now.

- **User Account Control:** Click the Turn On Now
  button. You need to restart Windows to complete your changes.

By following the five preceding steps, your computer will be
much safer than under any previous version of Microsoft
Windows.

The Security Center's four sections only let you flip an On
switch. For more advanced fiddling, look for their names atop
the Security Center's leftmost pane. A click on a name takes
you to that area's settings menu, where you can change how it
works or even turn it off.

In addition to using the Security Center, you may want to keep
on top of the latest security news. Microsoft lists virus alerts,
security bulletins, and other information in the security area
of its Web site (www.microsoft.com/security). There,
you can find out about the latest worms and viruses, as well
as some removal tools to fix infected computers (if the poor
PC is still able to connect to the Internet, that is).

Changing the firewall settings

Just about everybody has dropped his or her fork to pick up
the phone, only to hear a recorded sales pitch. Telemarketers
run programs that sequentially dial phone numbers until
somebody answers. Computer hackers run similar programs
that automatically try to break into every computer that's currently connected to the Internet.

Broadband Internet users are especially vulnerable because
their computers are constantly connected to the Internet.

That increases the chances that hackers will locate them and try to exploit any available vulnerability.

That's where Windows Firewall comes in. The firewall sits between your computer and the Internet, acting as an intelligent doorman. If something tries to connect and you or one of your programs didn't request it, the firewall refuses the connection.

Occasionally, however, you'll *want* another computer to interact with your computer over the Internet. You might be playing a multiplayer game, for example, or using a file-sharing program. To stop the firewall from blocking those programs, add their names to the firewall's exceptions list by following these steps:

1. **Choose Control Panel from the Start menu, click Security, and choose Security Center (shown in the margin).**

2. **Click the words Windows Firewall on the Security Center's left pane.**

   Click Continue if Vista's permissions screen nags you.

3. **Click the Exceptions tab.**

   Shown in Figure 4-3, Windows Firewall lists every program currently allowed to communicate through its firewall. (Windows Vista adds some of its programs automatically, so don't be surprised to see some already listed.)

4. **Click the Add Program button, select the program (or click Browse to locate the program), and click OK.**

   Almost all programs live in the Program Files folder on your C: drive; the program's name bears the same icon you see on its Start menu listing.

   The firewall adds your selected program to its Exceptions list and begins allowing other computers to connect to it.

In Step 4, make sure that a check mark appears in the Tell Me When Windows Firewall Blocks a Program box, as shown in Figure 4-3. When a program doesn't work correctly, that message lets you know that the firewall settings may be the culprit.

Figure 4-3: If the firewall blocks a program unnecessarily, add the program to the Exceptions list.

Here's some more helpful advice for working with firewall settings:

✔ Don't add programs to the Exceptions list unless you're *sure* that the firewall is the problem. Each time you add a program to the list, you're leaving your computer slightly more vulnerable.

✔ Using a laptop and connecting wirelessly to the Internet in a coffee shop, hotel, or other public place? Click the General tab in Step 3 and choose Block All Programs. That temporarily removes *all* your programs from the Exceptions list, providing the most security when computing in a public, wireless environment.

✔ If a program instructs you to "open a port" on the firewall, choose Add Port instead of Add Program in Step 4. Type the required port's name and number and then choose whether it's a TCP (Transmission Control Protocol) or UDP (User Datagram Protocol) port. Click OK to finish.

✔ If you think you've messed up the firewall's settings, it's easy to revert to its original settings. Click the Advanced tab in Step 3 and click the Restore Defaults button. Click the OK button, and the firewall removes every change you've made, letting you start from scratch.

Changing Windows Update settings

Whenever somebody figures out a way to break into Windows, Microsoft releases yet another patch to keep Windows users safe. Unfortunately, the bad folks find holes in Windows as quickly as Microsoft can patch them. The result? Microsoft ends up releasing a constant stream of patches.

In fact, the flow became so strong that many users couldn't keep up. Microsoft's solution is to make Windows Update work *automatically:* Whenever you go online, whether to check e-mail or browse the Web, your computer automatically visits Microsoft's Windows Update site and downloads any new patches in the background while you work.

When your computer's through downloading the new patches, it installs them at 3 a.m. to avoid disturbing your work. Occasionally, you are prompted to restart your computer the next morning to make the patches start working; other times, you don't even notice the action having taken place.

Vista's Security Center, covered earlier in this chapter, explains how to make sure Windows Update is up and running correctly and efficiently. But if you want to adjust its settings — perhaps not installing new patches until you've had a chance to review them — follow these steps:

1. **Click the Start button, choose All Programs, and choose Windows Update.**

   The Windows Update window appears.

2. **Choose Change Settings from the far left pane.**

   The settings page for Windows Update appears, as shown in Figure 4-4.

3. **Make your changes, then click OK.**

   Chances are, you won't need to make any changes. But if the 3 a.m. automatic installation time interferes with other software, or you happen to be a night owl, feel free to change the time.

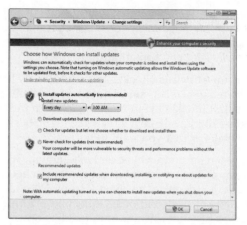

Figure 4-4: Make sure that you choose Install Updates Automatically.

 Some experienced computer users select the option marked Download Updates, but Let Me Choose Whether to Install Them. That option gives them a chance to review the incoming patches before installing them.

Avoiding viruses

When it comes to viruses, *everything* is suspect. Viruses travel not only in e-mail and programs, but also in screen savers, themes, toolbars, and other Windows add-ons. Because Vista doesn't include a built-in virus program, thus allowing you to choose your own, follow these rules to reduce your risk of infection:

✔ When shopping for an antivirus program, look for one that runs automatically in the background. If you don't yet have an antivirus program, open the Control Panel's Security icon, choose Security Center, and click the Malware Protection section's Find a Program button for free trial offers.

✔ Tell your antivirus program to scan everything you download, as well as anything that comes attached to or embedded in your e-mail or arrives through a messaging program.

✔ Only open attachments that you're expecting. If you receive something unexpected from a friend, don't open it. Instead, e-mail or call that person to see whether he or she *really* sent you something.

✔ Don't run two virus checkers simultaneously because they often quarrel. If you want to test a different program, first uninstall your existing one with the Control Panel's Programs icon. It's then safe to install another virus checker that you want to try out.

✔ Simply buying a virus checker isn't enough; you must also pay an annual fee to keep your virus checker smart enough to recognize the latest viruses. Without the most up-to-date virus definitions, virus checkers only detect older viruses, not the new ones heading down the pipe today. (The newest viruses always spread most quickly, causing the most damage.)

If you think you have a virus and you don't have an antivirus program, unplug your modem (or unplug it from the telephone line) before heading to the store and buying an antivirus program. Install and run the antivirus program *before* reconnecting your computer to the Internet. That stops your computer from infecting others before you're able to disinfect it.

McAfee offers a free virus-removal tool that removes more than 50 common viruses. Downloadable from `http://vil.nai.com/vil/stinger`, it's a handy tool for times of need.

Part II
Working with Programs and Files

The 5th Wave   By Rich Tennant

UBER-USER DWAYNE GRANTZ CHALKS UP BEFORE PUTTING WINDOWS VISTA THROUGH ITS PACES.

In this part . . .

*T*his part lets you put your knowledge of Vista's nuts and bolts from Part I to work. For example, I explain how to print, scan, and fax your work with Vista's strange new fax and scanning program.

And when some of your files wander (it's unavoidable), Chapter 6 explains how to unleash Vista's new robotic search hounds to track them down and bring them within reach.

In addition, this part covers how to find good stuff online while still keeping you and your computer safe. Finally, Chapter 9 gets you up to speed on the new features coming your way soon in Microsoft Office 2007.

Chapter 5

Playing with Programs and Documents

- -

In This Chapter
▶ Opening a program or document
▶ Creating a shortcut
▶ Cutting or copying and pasting
▶ Using Windows Vista's free programs

- -

*I*n Windows, *programs* are your tools: They let you add numbers, arrange words, and shoot spaceships. *Documents,* by contrast, are the things you create with programs: tax forms, heartfelt apologies, and high scores.

This chapter starts with the basics of opening programs, creating shortcuts, and cutting and pasting information between documents. Finally, it ends with a tour of Windows Vista's free programs.

Starting Programs and Connecting Them with the Right Files

Clicking the Start button presents the Start menu, the launching pad for your programs. The Start menu is strangely intuitive. For example, if it notices you've been making lots of

DVDs, the Start menu automatically moves the DVD Maker
program's icon to its front page for easy access, as shown in
Figure 5-1.

Figure 5-1: Click the Start button and then click the program you want
to open.

Don't see your favorite program on the Start menu's front
page? Click All Programs near the bottom of the Start menu.
The Start menu covers up its previously displayed icons with
an even *larger* list of programs and category-stuffed folders.
Still don't spot your program? Click some of the folders to
unveil even *more* programs stuffed inside.

When you spot your program, click its name. The program
opens onto the desktop, ready for work.

If your program doesn't seem to be living on the Start menu,
Windows Vista offers plenty of other ways to open a program,
including the following:

 ✓ Open the Documents folder from the Start menu and
   double-click the file you want to work on. The correct
   program automatically opens, with your chosen file
   in tow.

✔ Double-click a *shortcut* to the program. Shortcuts, which often sit on your desktop, are handy, disposable push buttons for launching files and folders. I describe how to create shortcuts later in this chapter.

✔ Click the program's icon on the Windows' Quick Launch toolbar — a small, handy strip of icons that resides next to the Start button.

✔ Right-click your desktop, choose New, and select the type of document you want to create. Windows Vista loads the right program for the job.

✔ Type the program's name in the Search box at the bottom of the Start menu and press Enter.

Windows offers other ways to open a program, but these methods usually get the job done.

Fortunately, most of the time, Windows Vista automatically knows which program should open which file. Double-click any file, and Windows tells the correct program to jump in and let you view its contents. But when Windows Vista gets confused, the problem lands in *your* lap.

The next two sections explain what to do when the wrong program opens your file or, even worse, *no* program offers to do the job.

The wrong program loads my file!

Double-clicking a document usually brings up the correct program — the same program you used to create that document. But sometimes the wrong program keeps jumping in, hijacking one of your documents. (Different brands of media players constantly fight over the right to play your music or videos, for example.)

When the wrong program suddenly begins opening your documents, here's how to make the *right* program open it instead:

1. **Right-click your problematic file and select Open With from the pop-up menu.**

   Windows names a few programs you've used to open that file in the past. The program listed first has *top billing* — it's the program that normally jumps into action when you double-click your file. (Chances are, the wrong program is currently sitting in that spot.)

2. **Choose the program you want to designate to open the file.**

   If you spot your favorite program, you *could* double-click it to open your file immediately. But that wouldn't prevent the same problem from recurring. The *next* step tackles that challenge.

   If Windows doesn't list your favorite program anywhere on its list, you have to hunt around for it. Click the Browse button and navigate to the folder containing the program you want. (*Hint:* Hover your mouse pointer over the folders, and Windows lists the program inside.) You should spot your favorite program's icon sitting in one of those folders.

3. **Click the Always Use the Selected Program to Open This Kind of File check box and click OK.**

   That box makes Windows return top-billing status to your selected program. For example, choosing Paint Shop Pro (and checking the Always box) tells Windows to make Paint Shop Pro open that type of file the next time (and every time, till you say otherwise) it's double-clicked.

Here are some additional tips for opening files:

✔ Sometimes you'll want to alternate between two programs when working on the same document. To do that, right-click the document, choose Open With, and select the program you need at that point in time.

✔ Sometimes you can't make your favorite program open a particular file because it simply doesn't know how. For example, Windows Media Player can usually play videos, *except* when they're stored in QuickTime, a format used by Microsoft's competition. Your only solution is to install QuickTime and use it to open that particular video.

No program will open my file!

It's frustrating when several programs fight to open your file. But it's even worse when *no program* ponies up to the task.

Double-clicking your file merely summons a cryptic error message.

If you already know the program needed to open your file, choose the second option: Select a Program From a List of Installed Programs. That summons a familiar window, letting you choose your program and then click OK to open the file.

But if you have no idea which program should open your mystery file, choose the Use the Web Service to Find the Correct Program button and click OK. Windows dashes off to the Internet in search of the right program. If you're lucky, Internet Explorer displays a Microsoft Web site. There, Microsoft identifies your file, describes its contents, and suggests a Web site for downloading a capable program.

Visit the Web site Microsoft suggests, download and install the program (after scanning it with a virus-checking program), and you've solved the file-opening problem.

Keep these helpful hints in mind when you're having trouble opening files:

✔ When you visit a Web site to download a suggested program like the QuickTime and RealPlayer movie players, you often find *two* versions: Free and Professional (expensive). The free version often works fine, so try it first.

✔ If you can't find *any* program that lets you open your file, you're simply stuck. You must contact the people who gave you that file and ask them what program you need to open it. Then, unfortunately, you'll probably have to buy that program's software.

Opening and Saving Documents

Like Tupperware, Windows Vista is a big fan of standardization. All Windows programs load their documents — often called *files* — exactly the same way:

1. **Click the word File on any program's *menu bar,* that row of staid words along the program's top. (No menu bar? Press Alt to reveal it.) When the File menu drops down, click Open.**

Windows gives you a sense of déjà vu with the Open box, shown in Figure 5-2: It looks (and works) just like your Documents folder.

There's one big difference, however: This time, your folder displays only files that your program knows how to open — it filters out all the others.

2. **See the list of documents inside the Open box in Figure 5-2? Point at your desired document, click the mouse, and click the Open button.**

The program opens the file and displays it on the screen.

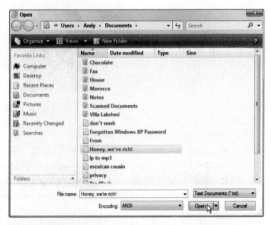

Figure 5-2: Double-click the filename you want to open or click once to select and then click the Open button.

Opening a file works this way in *any* Windows program, whether written by Microsoft, its corporate partners, or the teenager down the street.

The following items provide additional info for working with files:

✔ To speed things up, double-click a desired file's name; double-clicking opens it immediately, automatically closing the Open box.

✔ If your file isn't listed by name, start browsing by clicking the buttons shown along the left side of Figure 5-2. Click the Pictures folder, for example, to see files stored in that folder. Click Recently Changed to see files you've worked on recently; if you spot the one you want, pluck it from the list with a double-click.

✔ Whenever you open a file and change it, even by accidentally pressing the spacebar, Windows Vista assumes that you've changed the file for the better. If you try to close the file, Windows Vista cautiously asks whether you want to save your changes. If you changed the file with masterful wit, click Yes. If you made a mess or arrived here by mistake, click No or Cancel.

Saving means to send the work you've just created to a disk or hard drive for safekeeping. Unless you specifically save your work, your computer thinks that you've just been fiddling around for the past four hours. You must specifically tell the computer to save your work before it will safely store it.

When programmers fight over file types

When not fighting over fast food, programmers fight over *formats* — ways to pack information into a file. To accommodate the format wars, some programs have a special feature that lets you open files stored in several different types of formats.

For example, look at the drop-down list box in the bottom right corner of Figure 5-2. It currently lists Text Documents (*.txt) format, the format used by Notepad. So, the Open box displays only files stored in Notepad's format. To see files stored in *other* formats, click in that box and choose a different format. The Open box quickly updates its list to show files from that newly selected format.

And how can you see a list of *all* your folder's files in that menu, regardless of their content? Choose All Files from the drop-down list box. You'll see all your files, but your program probably won't be able to open all of them, and will choke or complain if it tries.

Notepad lists digital photos in its All Files menu, for example. But if you try to open a photo, Notepad dutifully displays the photo as obscure coding symbols. (If you ever mistakenly open a photo in a program and *don't* see the photo, don't try to save what you've opened. If the program is like Notepad, it will ruin it. Simply turn tail and exit immediately to find a program that will oblige your request.)

What's the difference between Save and Save As?

Huh? Save as *what?* A chemical compound? Naw, the Save As command just gives you a chance to save your work with a different name and in a different location.

Suppose that you open the *Ode to Tina* file in your Documents folder and change a few sentences. You want to save your new changes, but you don't want to lose the original words, either. Preserve *both* versions by selecting Save As and typing the new name, *Tentative Additions to Ode to Tina.*

When you're saving something for the *first* time, the Save and Save As commands are identical: Both make you choose a fresh name and location for your work.

Thanks to Microsoft's snapping leather whips, the same Save command appears in all Windows Vista programs, no matter what programmer wrote them. Click File from the top menu, choose Save, and save your document in your Documents folder or to your desktop for easy retrieval later.

If you're saving something for the first time, Windows Vista asks you to think up a name for your document. Type something descriptive using only letters, numbers, and spaces between the words. Vista adds the applicable program file extension automatically.

The following list provides more tips for saving those precious documents of yours:

- ✔ Choose descriptive and relevant filenames for your work. Windows Vista gives you 255 characters to work with, so a file named *June Report on Squeegee Sales* is easier to locate than one named *Stuff.*

- ✔ You can save files to any folder, CD, or even a memory card. But files are much easier to find down the road when they stay in the Documents folder. (Feel free to save a *second* copy onto a CD as a backup.)

✔ Most programs can save files directly to a CD. Choose
Save from the File menu and then choose your CD burner.
Put a CD (preferably one that's not already filled) into
your CD-writing drive to start the process.

✔ If you're working on something important (and most
things are), choose the program's Save command every
few minutes. Or use the Ctrl+S keyboard shortcut (while
holding down the Ctrl key, press the S key). Programs
make you choose a name and location for a file when you
first save it; subsequent saves are much speedier.

Taking the Shortcuts

Some items are buried *way* too deeply inside of your computer, which makes quick access a difficult task. If you're tired
of meandering through the woods to find your favorite program, folder, disk drive, document, or even a Web site, create
a *shortcut* — an icon push button that takes you directly to the
object of your desires.

Because a shortcut is a mere push button that launches something else, you can move, delete, and copy shortcuts without
harming the original. They're safe, convenient, and easy to
create. And they're easy to tell apart from the original,
because they have a little arrow lodged in their bottom-left
corner, such as the FreeCell shortcut shown in the margin.

Follow these instructions to create shortcuts to these always
popular Windows doodads:

✔ **Folders or Documents:** Right-click the folder, choose
Send To, and select the Desktop (Create Shortcut)
option. When the shortcut appears on your desktop,
drag and drop it wherever you find most handy.

✔ **Web sites:** See the little icon in front of the Web site's
address in Internet Explorer's Address bar? Drag and
drop that little icon to your desktop — or anyplace else.
(It helps to drag one of Internet Explorer's window edges
inward a bit first so you can see part of your desktop.)
You can also add Web sites to Internet Explorer's handy
list of Favorites.

✔ **Anything on your Start menu:** Right-click the object and choose Copy. Then right-click where you want the short-cut to reside and choose Paste Shortcut.

✔ **Nearly anything else:** Drag and drop the object to a new place while holding down your right mouse button. When you let go of the mouse button, choose Create Shortcuts Here, and the shortcut appears.

✔ **Disk drives:** Open the Computer folder, right-click the drive you want, and choose Create Shortcut. Then accept Windows' gracious offer to place a shortcut to that drive on your desktop, as shown in Figure 5-3.

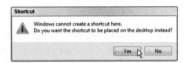

Shortcut

Windows cannot create a shortcut here.
Do you want the shortcut to be placed on the desktop instead?

Yes   No

Figure 5-3: Accept Windows' kind offer of placing the shortcut on the desktop.

Here are some more shortcuts for using shortcuts:

✔ For quick CD burning, put a shortcut to your CD burner on your desktop. Burning files to CD becomes as simple as dragging and dropping them onto the CD burner's new shortcut. (Double-click the CD burner's shortcut to dic-tate settings and begin burning.)

✔ Feel free to move shortcuts from place to place but *don't* move the items they launch. If you do, the shortcut won't be able to find the item, causing Windows to panic, searching (usually vainly) for the moved goods.

✔ If you create a shortcut but the icon *doesn't* have that little arrow in its bottom left corner, *stop.* Calmly hold down the Ctrl button and press Z to reverse your action. Then try again.

✔ Want to see what program a shortcut will launch? Right-click on the shortcut, choose Properties, and click Open File Location (if available). The shortcut quickly takes you to its leader.

The Absolutely Essential Guide to Cutting, Copying, and Pasting

Windows Vista took a tip from the kindergartners and made *cut and paste* play an integral part of life. You can electronically *cut* or *copy* just about anything and then *paste* somewhere else with little fuss and even less mess.

Windows programs are designed to work together and share information, making it fairly easy to put a scanned map onto your party invitation fliers. You can move files by cutting or copying them from one place and pasting them into another. And you can easily cut and paste paragraphs to different locations within a program.

The beauty of Windows Vista is that, with all those windows on-screen at the same time, you can easily grab bits and pieces from any of them and paste all the parts into a brand new window.

Don't overlook copying and pasting for the small stuff. Copying a name and address from your Contacts program is much quicker than typing it into your letter by hand. Or, when somebody e-mails you a Web address, copy and paste it directly into Internet Explorer's Address bar. It's as easy to copy most items displayed on Web sites, too (much to the dismay of many professional photographers).

In compliance with the Don't Bore Me with Details Department, here's a quick guide to the three basic steps used for cutting, copying, and pasting:

1. **Select the item to cut or copy: a few words, a file, a Web address, or any other item.**

2. **Right-click your selection and choose Cut or Copy from the menu, depending on your needs.**

   Use *Cut* when you want to *move* something. Use *Copy* when you want to duplicate something, leaving the original both intact and in its current location.

   Keyboard shortcut: Hold down Ctrl and press X to cut or C to copy.

3. Right-click the item's destination and choose Paste.

You can right-click inside a document, folder, or nearly any other place.

Keyboard shortcut: Hold down Ctrl and press V to paste.

After you've selected something, cut it or copy it *immediately.* If you absentmindedly click the mouse someplace else, your highlighted text or file reverts to its boring self, and you're forced to start over.

Windows Vista's Free Programs!

Windows Vista, the fanciest Windows version yet, comes with oodles of free programs, such as Media Player and Mail. These freebies make customers happy and make the European Antitrade Commission flap their long black robes.

This section merely focuses on Windows Vista's most useful freebies: its WordPad and Notepad word processors, the Calendar scheduling program, Character Map, and Paint.

Writing letters with WordPad

WordPad is nowhere near as fancy as some of the more expensive word processors on the market. It can't create tables or multiple columns, like the ones in newspapers or newsletters, nor can you double-space your reports. Forget the spell checker, too.

WordPad is, however, great for quick letters, simple reports, and other basic stuff. You can change the fonts, too. And because all Windows users have WordPad on their computers, anything you create in WordPad can be read by 90 percent of other computer owners.

To give WordPad a whirl, choose All Programs from the Start menu, choose Accessories, and click WordPad.

If you've just ditched your typewriter for Windows, remember this: On an electric typewriter, you have to press the Return key at the end of each line, or else you start typing off the edge of the paper. Computers avoid that. They automatically drop down a line and continue the sentence. (Tech Hipsters call this phenomenon *word wrap.*)

Jotting down notes with Notepad

Use WordPad for letters that you want other people to see. Notepad, on the other hand, works best for stuff you're going to keep for yourself. Like its name, it's designed for typing notes to save on the fly.

To open the Notepad feature, choose All Programs from the Start menu, choose Accessories, and click Notepad.

Unfortunately, Notepad tosses you into instant confusion: When you start typing, the sentences head right off the edge of the window and out of sight. To turn those single-line, run-away sentences into normal paragraphs, choose Word Wrap from the Format menu. Windows Vista remembers your preference and *wraps* the lines to fit the page the next time you reach for Notepad.

Another warning: Unlike most word processors, Notepad doesn't print exactly what you see on-screen. Instead, it prints according to the margins you set in Page Setup from the File menu. This quirk can lead to unpredictable results. Stick with WordPad for documents you want to print.

Keeping appointments with Calendar

Vista tosses a new program not found in Windows XP into the mix: Calendar. Just like it sounds, Calendar is a full-fledged scheduling program that replaces hastily scribbled sticky notes on the refrigerator. Fire it up by clicking the Start menu, choosing All Programs, and selecting Windows Calendar.

Shown in Figure 5-4, Calendar presents a monthly calendar on the left side, your day's appointments in the middle, and the highlighted appointment's details on the right.

Figure 5-4: Vista's Calendar shows the appointments of you and your friends, making it easier to plan events.

To add an appointment, click a day on the calendar, click the time of the appointment, type the description, and start filling out the additional details on the right.

The beauty of Calendar is the way it lets you share appointments by publishing them to your Web site where friends and relatives can automatically *subscribe* to them, meaning Calendar will download and display them automatically.

The downside of Calendar is that you have no excuse for being late anymore.

Anybody who's used Microsoft's e-mail program, Outlook, will be well acquainted with Calendar, as it duplicates many of those features and can share its calendars. Vista's Calendar can also share calendars with your Mac friends who use iCal for their appointments. For a real downer, you may be able to share your calendar from work as well — ask your office network guru.

Finding symbols like © with Character Map

Character Map lets you insert common symbols and foreign characters into your current document, giving your documents that extra *coup de grâce*. The handy little program displays a box like the one shown in Figure 5-5, listing every available character and symbol.

Figure 5-5: Character Map finds symbols and foreign characters to place in your work.

For example, follow these steps to insert the copyright character — © — somewhere in your work:

1. **Click the Start menu, choose All Programs, select Accessories, choose System Tools, and select Character Map.**

   Make sure that your current font — the name for the style of your letters — appears in the Font box.

   If the font you're using in your document isn't showing, click the Font box's down arrow and then scroll down and click your font when it appears in the drop-down list.

2. **Scan the Character Map box until you see the symbol you're after; then pounce on that character with a double-click.**

The symbol appears in the Characters to Copy box.

3. **Right-click in the document where you want the symbol to appear and choose Paste.**

The symbol appears, conveniently using the same font as your document.

Drawing and editing photos with Paint

A very basic graphics program, Paint creates simple drawings. If it's the only graphics program you have, you'll probably use it mostly for cropping photos. Open the Start menu, choose All Programs, and select Accessories to find Paint's listing.

Keep in mind that with such limited capabilities, Paint is better for quick touch-ups than ground-zero creations.

In addition, you can paste anything you create or edit in Paint into almost any other Windows Vista program. Paint enables you to add text and numbers to graphics, so you can add street names to maps copied from the Internet, put labels inside your drawings, or add the vintage year to your wine labels.

Paint opens and saves files in BMP, JPG, GIF, TIF, and PNG formats. Use JPG for photographs, TIF for production-quality work, and PNG or GIF for Web buttons. Stay away from BMP, an oddball format from days gone by. (BMP files are *huge,* making them too awkward to e-mail or store.)

Chapter 6

Briefly Lost, but Quickly Found

*S*ooner or later, Windows Vista gives you that head-scratching feeling. "Golly," you say, as you tug on your mouse cord, "that stuff was *right there* a second ago. Where did it go?" When Windows Vista starts playing hide-and-seek with your information, this chapter tells you where to search and how to make it stop playing foolish games.

This chapter shares some of Vista's new tricks with old-school tips to find those things that suddenly disappear: windows on a crowded desktop, files lost in a sea of file names, photos no longer found in your digital shoebox, along with those lost applications, e-mails, songs, and miscellaneous documents.

Finding Lost Windows

Windows Vista works more like a spike memo holder than an actual desktop. Every time you open a new window, you toss another piece of information onto the spike. The window on top is easy to spot, but how do you reach the windows lying beneath it?

If you can see any part of a buried window's edge or corner, a well-placed click will fetch it, bringing it to the top.

 When your window is completely buried, look at the desktop's taskbar — that strip along your monitor's bottom edge. (If the taskbar is missing as well, retrieve it with a press of the Windows key, shown in the margin.) Click your missing window's name on the taskbar to dredge it back to the top.

Still missing? Try Vista's fancy new Flip 3D view by holding down the Windows key and pressing Tab. Shown in Figure 6-1, Vista does a magician's shuffle with your windows, letting you see them hanging in the air. While holding down the Windows key, keep pressing Tab (or rolling your mouse's scroll wheel) until your lost window rises to the front of the pack. Let go of the Windows key to place that window at the top of your desktop.

Figure 6-1: Hold down the Windows key and press Tab repeatedly to cycle through your windows; release the Windows key to drop the top window onto the desktop.

If your older PC can't handle Vista's 3D View (or if your newer PC's graphics card isn't up to snuff), hold down Alt and press Tab for the two-dimensional substitute that works the same or maybe even better. While holding down Alt, keep pressing Tab until Vista highlights your window; let go of Alt to place your newfound window atop your desktop.

If you're convinced that a window is open but you still can't find it, spread all your windows across the desktop: Right-click the taskbar along the desktop's bottom and choose Show Windows Side By Side from the menu. It's a last resort, but perhaps you'll spot your missing window in the lineup.

Finding Lost Files, Folders, Music, Photos, and More

It rarely takes more than a few minutes to find information on the Internet, even though you're searching through millions of PCs worldwide. But try to find a document on your PC, and you could spend days — if it ever turns up at all.

To solve the search problem, Vista took a tip from Internet search engines like Google and created an index of your PC's main files. To find your missing file, open the Start menu and click in the Search box along the bottom.

Start typing the first few letters of a word, name, or phrase that appears somewhere inside the file you're looking for. As soon as you begin typing, Vista's Start menu begins listing matches. With each letter you type, Vista whittles down the list. After you type enough letters, your lost document floats alone to the top of the list, ready to be opened with a double-click.

For example, typing the first few letters of **Thelonious** into the Start menu's Search box, shown in Figure 6-2, brought up every Thelonious Monk song on my PC.

When you spot your file, click its name on the Start menu to open it. Or right-click its name and choose Open File Location from the pop-up menu to see the folder where your file's been hiding away.

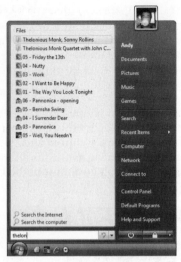

Figure 6-2: Type a few words from your document, e-mail, or music file, and Vista locates the files, placing the closest matches at the top.

The following items offer other hints to help you find just the file you're looking for:

✔ Vista's Index includes every file in your Documents, Pictures, Music and Videos folders. That makes it more important than ever to store your files in those folders. (Vista doesn't let you search through files stored in accounts of *other* people who may be using your PC.)

✔ The index also includes any files strewn across your desktop, the text on every Web site you've visited in the past few weeks, recently deleted files languishing in your Recycle Bin, people you've entered as contacts, and all your e-mail. (Vista also indexes any files you're sharing in your Public folder — the folder that other PCs can access from a network.)

✔ If you're searching for a common word and Vista turns up too many files, limit your search by typing a short phrase: **Thelonious Monk played Tuesday night**. The more letters of a phrase you type, the better your chances of pinpointing a particular file.

✔ When searching for files, begin typing with the *first* letter of a word or phrase: **t** for Thelonious, for example. If you type **onious**, Vista won't find Thelonious, even though Thelonious contains that string of letters.

✔ The Search Box ignores capital letters. It considers *Bee* and *bee* to be the same insect.

✔ Want to route your search to the Internet rather than your PC? After typing your word or phrase, click the words Search the Internet, shown directly above the Search box in Figure 6-2. Vista sends your search to the search engine you've chosen in Internet Explorer.

Finding a missing file in a folder

The Start menu's Search box probes Vista's entire index, making sure that it's looked everywhere. But that's overkill when you're poking around inside a folder, looking randomly for a missing file. To solve the "sea of filenames in a folder" problem, Vista placed a Search box in every folder's upper right corner. That Search box limits your search to files within that *particular* folder.

To find a missing file within a specific folder, click inside that folder's Search box and begin typing a word or short phrase from your missing file. As you begin typing letters and words, Vista begins filtering out files that don't contain that word or phrase. It keeps narrowing down the candidates until the folder displays only a few files, including, hopefully, your runaway file.

When a folder's Search box locates too many possible matches, bring in some other helping hands: Choose Details from the folder's Views button, which lines up your files in one column, as shown in Figure 6-3. The first column, Name, lists the name of each file; the adjacent columns list specific details about each file.

See the column headers such as Name, Date Modified, and Authors atop each column? Click any of those headers to sort your files by that term. Here's how to sort by some of the column headers in your Documents folder:

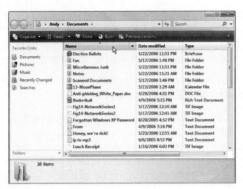

Figure 6-3: Viewing files in Details view lets you sort your files by name, making them easier to find.

✔ **Name:** Know the first letter of your file's name? Then click here to sort your files alphabetically. You can then pluck your file from the list. Click Name again to reverse the sort order.

✔ **Date Modified:** When you remember the approximate date you last changed a document, click the Date Modified header. Your newest files now appear at the top of the list, making them easy to locate. (Clicking Date Modified again reverses the order, a handy way to weed out old files you may no longer need.)

✔ **Type:** This header sorts files by their contents: All your photos are grouped together, for example, as are all your Word documents. It's a handy way to find a few stray photos swimming in a sea of text files.

✔ **Authors:** Microsoft Word and some other programs tack your name onto your work. A click on this label alphabetically sorts the files by their creator's name.

✔ **Tags:** Vista often lets you assign tags to your documents. Adding the tags Moldy Cheese Photos to that pungent photo session lets you retrieve those pictures by either typing their tags or sorting a folder's files by their tags.

Folders usually display about five columns of details, but you can add more columns. In fact, you can sort files by their word count, song length, photo size, creation date, and dozens of other details. To see a list of available detail columns, right-click an existing label along a column's top.

When the drop-down menu appears, select More to see the Choose Details dialog box. Click to put a checkmark next to each new detail column you'd like to see and click OK.

Finding lost photos

Windows Vista indexes your e-mail down to the last word, but it can't tell the difference between your Yosemite photos and your photo shoot at Dog Beach. When it comes to photos, the ID work lies in your hands, and these three tips make the chore as easy as possible:

- ✔ **Tags:** When you connect your camera to your PC, Vista graciously offers to copy your photos to your PC. While copying, Vista also asks you to "Tag these pictures." That's your big chance to type a *tag* — a computer term for a descriptive word or short phrase. Tags give Vista something to index, making the photos easier to retrieve later.

- ✔ **Store shooting sessions in separate folders.** Vista's photo importing program automatically creates a new folder, named after the tag you chose, to store each session. But if you're using some other program to dump photos, be sure to create a new folder for each session. Then name the folder with a short description of your session: Sushi Dinner, Parboiling Potatoes, or Truffle Hunt.

Have you stumbled onto a massive folder that's a huge mishmash of digital photos? Here's a quick sorting trick: Repeatedly click View from the folder's top menu until the photos morph into identifiable thumbnails. Then, right-click a blank part of the folder, choose Sort By, and select either Date Modified or Date Taken. Sorting the photos by date usually lines them up in the order in which you snapped them, turning chaos into organization.

- ✔ **Rename your photos.** Instead of leaving your Belize vacation photos named DSCM1045, DSCM1046, and so on, give them meaningful names: Select all the files in your folder by holding down Ctrl and pressing A. Then, right-click the first picture, choose Rename, and type **Belize**. Windows names them as Belize, Belize (2), Belize (3), and so on.

Following these three simple rules helps keep your photo collection from becoming a jumble of files.

Be *sure* to back up your digital photos to a portable hard drive, CDs, DVDs, or another backup method. If they're not backed up, you'll lose your family history when your PC's hard drive eventually crashes.

Finding other computers on a network

Most people use a network every day without knowing it: Every time you check your e-mail, your PC connects to another PC to grab your waiting messages. A *network* is simply a group of connected PCs that can share things, such as your Internet connection, files, or a printer.

Much of the time you don't need to care about the other PCs on your network. But when you want to find a connected PC, perhaps to grab the files from the PC in your family room, Vista is happy to help.

To find a PC on your network, choose Network from the Start menu. Vista lists every PC that's connected to your own PC. To browse files on any of those PCs, just double-click their names, as shown in Figure 6-4.

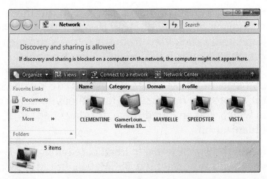

Figure 6-4: To find computers connected to your PC through a network, click the Start menu and choose Network.

Finding information on the Internet

When Vista comes up short while digging for information in your PC, tell it to search the Internet instead. That's easy enough to do in the Start menu's Search box; just click, type in your words, and click Search the Internet above the Search box.

Routing a folder's Search box to the Internet takes an extra step: Click the little arrow to the right of the Search box in the folder's window. When the drop-down menu appears, choose Search the Internet.

Whether the search comes from the Start menu's Search box or a folder's Search box, Vista sends your query to the search engine normally used by Internet Explorer's Search box.

Chapter 7

Getting Stuff Into and Out of Your Computer

*O*ccasionally, you want to slip something out of your PC's whirling electrons and onto something more permanent: A piece of paper.

This chapter tackles that job by explaining all you need to know about printing. I also explain how to turn your computer into a free fax machine with Vista's fax program. Now you can delete those junk faxes before they waste your roll of fax paper. Finally, the last section explains how to scan something with your scanner.

Printing Your Masterpiece

Windows Vista shuttles your work off to the printer in any of a half-dozen different ways. Chances are, you'll be using these three methods most often:

✔ Choose Print from your program's File menu.

✔ Right-click your document icon and choose Print.

✔ Drag and drop a document's icon onto your printer's icon.

If a dialog box appears, click the OK button; Windows Vista immediately begins sending your pages to the printer. Take a minute or so to refresh your coffee. If the printer is turned on (and still has paper and ink), Windows handles everything automatically. If your coffee cup is still full, keep on working or playing FreeCell. Windows prints your work in the background.

If the printed pages don't look quite right — perhaps the information doesn't fit on the paper correctly or it looks faded — then it's time to fiddle around with the print settings or perhaps change the paper quality.

Here are a few useful ideas to save you time when printing:

- ✔ If you stumble on a particularly helpful page in the Windows Help system, right-click inside the topic or page and choose Print. Windows prints a copy for you to tape to your wall or save in this book.

- ✔ For quick 'n' easy access to your printer, right-click your printer's icon and choose Create Shortcut. Click Yes to confirm, and Windows Vista puts a shortcut to your printer on your desktop. To print things, just drag and drop the file's icon onto your printer's new shortcut. (You can find your printer's icon by opening the Control Panel from the Start menu and choosing Printers.)

- ✔ To print a bunch of documents quickly, select *all* their icons. Then right-click the selected icons and choose Print. Windows Vista quickly shuttles all of them to the printer where they emerge on paper, one after the other.

Just realized you sent the wrong 26-page document to the printer? So you panic and flip the printer's off switch. Unfortunately, most printers automatically pick up where they left off when you turn them back on.

To purge your mistake from the printer's memory, double-click your Printer's icon (which sometimes sits near the taskbar's clock) to reveal the *print queue*. Right-click your mistaken document and choose Cancel to end the job. Now, when you turn your printer back on, it won't keep printing that same darn document.

Troubleshooting your printer

If you can't print your document, are you *sure* that the printer is turned on, plugged into the wall, full of paper, and connected securely to your computer with a cable?

If you answered "Yes" to all these questions, try plugging the printer into different outlets, turning it on, and seeing if its power light comes on. If the light stays off, your printer's power supply is probably blown. Printers are almost always cheaper to replace than repair. But if you've grown fond of your printer, grab an estimate from a repair shop before discarding it.

If the printer's power light beams brightly, check these things before giving up:

✔ Make sure that a sheet of paper hasn't jammed itself inside the printer somewhere. (A steady pull usually extricates jammed paper.)

✔ Does your inkjet printer still have ink in its cartridges? Does your laser printer have toner? Try printing a test page: Click the Start menu, open the Control Panel, and choose Printers. Right-click your printer's icon, choose Properties, and click the Print Test Page button to see whether the computer and printer can talk to each other.

✔ Try updating the printer's *driver,* the little program that helps it talk to Windows Vista. Visit the printer manufacturer's Web site, download the newest driver for your particular printer model, and run its installation program.

Finally, here are a couple of tips to help you protect your printer and cartridges:

✔ Turn off your printer when you're not using it. Inkjet printers, especially, should be turned off when they're not in use. The heat tends to dry the cartridges, shortening their life.

✔ Don't unplug your inkjet printer to turn it off. Always use the on/off switch. The switch ensures that the cartridges slide back to their home positions, which keeps them from drying out or clogging.

Sending and Receiving Faxes

Windows Vista's Fax and Scan does away with the rolls of fax paper you've needed in the past by letting your PC serve double-duty as a fax machine. Instead of printing your documents and running them through a traditional fax machine, you send a fax by telling your program to print the document through Vista's fax program. (To simplify things, Vista lists its fax program as an available printer in your program's menus.)

Type the recipient's fax number, fill out a simple cover page form, push a button, and your document appears on somebody else's fax machine a few minutes later.

When somebody sends you a fax, your computer answers the call, receives the fax, and displays it on your screen. (Feel free to print it, if necessary.)

You need four things to send or receive faxes with Windows Vista:

- ✔ **A modem with faxing capabilities.** Cable modems and DSL modems can't send faxes — that's a perk reserved for dial-up modems.

- ✔ **A dial-up phone line.** Cell phones won't work.

- ✔ **Vista's fax program.** Unfortunately, Windows Vista Home Basic and Home Premium don't include the Fax and Scan program. Microsoft reserved the privilege for Vista's Business, Enterprise, and Ultimate versions.

- ✔ **A scanner.** You need a scanner to fax items that aren't already inside your computer: coffee shop menus, for example. You won't need a scanner if you fax only computer files, though.

You can send faxes without the modem and dial-up phone line if your business runs a *fax server:* a networked PC specially set up to send faxes as attachments through e-mail.

Microsoft limits its fax program to Windows XP Professional, but left it as an uninstalled bonus item on Windows XP Home retail CDs. There's no way of knowing whether Vista's Home versions will also include the fax program as an uninstalled bonus item until Vista's consumer version arrives in early 2007.

Setting up your computerized fax machine

Setting up a *real* fax machine starts with the boring stuff: Plugging it in, punching in the current date and your fax number, and telling it when to answer. Windows Vista's virtual fax machine starts with a boring setup ritual as well: setting up a fax account.

Unlike Windows XP's fax program, Windows Vista combines the fax program with a scanning program — which makes sense, because you'll often scan things in order to fax them. Unfortunately, the combination somehow made Vista's fax program more awkward than Windows XP's fax program.

Setting up Windows Fax and Scan

Before you can begin faxing documents, you must set up the program. Similar to setting up a printer, these steps place a little fax machine icon in Vista's Print menus. Sending a fax becomes as simple as choosing the fax machine with any program's Print menu.

The first time you try to send a fax, Vista asks you to set up the program by following the steps below. (To set up the program in advance, open Windows Fax and Scan from the Start menu's All Programs area, and click the New Fax button.)

1. **Choose your type of fax connection.**

   To send faxes through your PC's built-in modem, choose Fax Modem Connection.

   To send faxes through your business' fax server, choose Windows Fax Server Connection.

2. **Choose a name for your account and click Create.**

   This name lets you choose these settings down the road, when you're ready to send a fax. Leave the Default Fax Account button checked.

   If an ominous message asks whether you should keep blocking Microsoft Windows Fax and Scan program, click Unblock. That keeps the pesky firewall from interfering with your fax.

You need to set up your new computerized fax machine before you can send or receive faxes.

Sending a fax directly from a program

Think of Vista's fax program as a printer. Anything you can print can now be faxed: a letter, map, drawing, spreadsheet, or even a menu from the corner deli's Web site. (To send something you've scanned, see this chapter's scanning section.) Follow these steps to transform a file in your PC into a paper fax in the tray of somebody's fax machine.

1. **Create your document and then choose Print from the program's File menu.**

   For example, to fax a letter from your word processor, choose Print — just as if you were sending it to the printer.

   If you don't spot a File or Print option, you may need to press your Alt key to reveal the program's hidden menus.

2. **When the Print dialog box appears, choose the fax as your printer and click Print (or OK).**

   The New Fax window appears.

3. **Fill out the New Fax window.**

   The fax window looks and acts much like an e-mail window with an attachment — your fax. The difference is that the recipient's fax machine spits out the attachment as the fax and the e-mailed text as the cover letter.

   Fill out these parts of the New Fax window, shown in Figure 7-1.

   • **Recipient:** Click the To button to select the recipient's name and fax number from your address book — the same one used by your e-mail program. Add as many recipients as you'd like, just as if you're sending e-mails to several people.

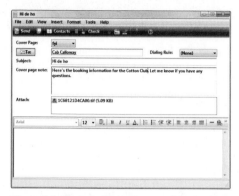

Figure 7-1: Click the To button to select the fax recipient and then type a brief cover letter.

- **Cover page note:** Choose a type of cover page from the Cover Page menu and then type exactly what you want to see on the cover letter. (The cover pages options are the same as in Windows XP, and Generic works fine for most faxes.)

- **Message body:** If you're sending the information to a person who uses Vista's fax program, Vista won't fax it. Instead, it *e-mails* the fax to their Inbox as an attachment. Type your e-mail message into the message body area at the bottom of the window.

4. **Click the Send button.**

Vista immediately whisks the fax to the fax number of the people you've listed in Step 3.

Want to send the fax during the evening, when the rates are cheaper? Choose Fax Options on the Tools menu. There, you can schedule the fax to be sent anytime you want.

Because Vista no longer walks you through the following necessary setup steps, consider tweaking these additional settings to ease your faxing life:

✔ Choose Sender Information from the Tools menu in the Windows Fax and Scan program. There, you can fill out your name and fax number as it should appear on your fax's accompanying cover letter. Stick with your name and fax number; you don't want to send your address and other personal information to *everybody.*

✔ To look up fax numbers or quickly add them to your contacts list, choose Address Book on the Tools menu.

✔ Don't forget the Forward as E-mail button along the program's menu bar. As fax machines go the way of the telegraph, more people want their faxes e-mailed to them. This button lets you e-mail a received fax to other people, neatly bypassing fax machines and their ugly rolls of paper.

Receiving a fax

If you hooked up your fax modem to a *dedicated* phone line — a line separate from your voice line — tell the fax program to answer incoming faxes automatically. When the phone rings, your computer answers, receives, and saves the fax and heralds its arrival by placing a pop-up message on your screen.

To tell Vista to answer incoming faxes automatically, open Windows Fax and Scan from the Start menu's All Programs area, and choose Fax Settings from the Tools menu.

When the screen shown in Figure 7-2 appears, click in the box marked Enable Device to Answer the Phone and Receive Faxes and then click Automatically Answer After 1 Ring, as shown in Figure 7-2.

Figure 7-2: If your PC has its own phone line, tell the fax to answer automatically.

If your PC shares its fax line with your voice line, however,
filling out the page in Figure 7-2 becomes more difficult: You
don't want your PC to miss an incoming fax, but you don't
want a whiny fax machine butting in on your voice calls. Here
are some ways to deal with sharing one line with your fax
machine:

✔ If you choose *Manual Answer,* every incoming phone call
brings a pop-up window to your screen. If you pick up
the phone and hear a fax machine on the other end, click
Answer Now in the pop-up window to begin receiving the
fax. This option works best for people who stay close to
their computers.

✔ If you choose *Automatically Answer after X rings,* the program answers *only* after the number of rings you choose.
Choose 5 rings, for example, and you have time to pick
up the phone and start your conversation without inter-
ruption from the fax machine. If you hear a fax tone
instead of a voice, simply hang up. The fax machine will
call back a minute or so later, and you'll know not to pick
up the phone.

✔ If your fax program won't answer your incoming faxes,
you need to choose Enable Device to Answer the Phone
and Receive Faxes, shown in Figure 7-2. Then tell the fax
to answer either manually or automatically — whichever
suits your needs.

Scanning a Photo, Letter, or Receipt

Most scanners and digital cameras come with their own
software — a strange, bulky bundle of commands for you to
try and remember. Fortunately, you usually don't have to
install or use that software because most cameras and scanners are Windows Vista compatible. Windows Vista's built-in
scanning tools can scan images and grab digital photos.
Even if you've been using the software packaged with your
scanner or camera, you may find Windows Vista's tools easier
to figure out.

Scanning with the Scanning and Camera Wizard

After you've hooked up your scanner to your PC, the following steps show you how to begin scanning anything: photos, letters, lunch receipts, or the cold cuts menu from that Italian deli down the street.

Before scanning, always clean the scanner's glass thoroughly with a lint-free cloth. Even the tiniest dust can appear on the scan. Also wipe any dust off the object you're scanning.

1. **Lift your scanner's cover, place the photo or letter on the glass, and close the cover.**

   Place the paper face down in the top-right corner, pushed up against the edges of the scanner bed.

   If you don't align your scanned photos or letters against the corner, the resulting scan will tilt to one side, making for weird prints. Close the scanner lid carefully to keep from scooting the paper to one side.

2. **Open the Windows Fax and Scan program.**

   Click the Start menu, choose All Programs, and select Windows Fax and Scan. (The program's icon is in the margin.)

3. **Select the Scans button, if necessary.**

   The Windows Fax and Scan program toggles between two views, one for scanning and one for faxing. A pair of little blue buttons in the program's bottom-left corner lets you switch between the two parts of the program.

   If you see the fax menu across the top, listing words like New Fax or Receive Fax Now, click the Scans button to switch to the scanning menu.

4. **Click the New Scan button, click your scanner's icon from the list, and click OK.**

   To accommodate the handful of people with more than one scanner attached to their PC, Vista asks everybody to click their scanner's icon from a list.

5. Choose any desired scanning options from the list.

The New Scan window shown in Figure 7-3 appears, offering several options for scanning. The most important choices fall in the Color Format and Resolution categories.

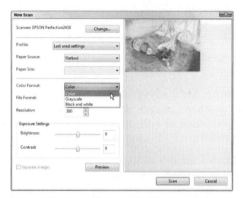

Figure 7-3: Choose Color from the Color Format menu for most scans.

Color Format: You have three choices:

- **Color:** The usual choice for most scans, it's the obvious choice for anything containing colors.

- **Grayscale:** Use this setting mostly for scanning black-and-white photos because it picks up different shades of gray. (It sometimes works well for scanning text as well.)

- **Black and white:** This option separates everything into only two colors: black or white. That makes it perfect for line drawings and very clearly printed text, but not much else.

Resolution: This determines the *sharpness* of an image — how well it looks onscreen and when printed. Although 150-to-300 works fine for most scans, this chapter's next section covers resolution in more detail.

Keep in mind that different scanners offer different options. Your scanner's screen may not look exactly like Figure 7-3.

6. Click the Scan button.

Vista scans your image and adds the scan to the program's list of scanned items. The following buttons along the menu bar let you do the following things with any fax on the list:

Forward as Fax: This button heralds the program's Fax area (described earlier in this section), which lets you fax your scan to somebody in your address book.

Forward as E-mail: Click here to e-mail your scanned image as an attachment.

Save As: Normally, your faxes stay trapped inside the Fax and Scan program. To copy them to another folder for reference or editing, choose Save As. (Save them in your Picture folder for easy access.)

Print: When you need a paper copy of a scan, choose Print from the File menu.

Keep in mind that unlike printers, most scanners can't be shared on a network. In addition, always remember to lock a scanner into place before moving it someplace. (Most scanners have a little knob on one side that locks it in place, preventing damage to its internal mechanisms.)

Choosing the right scanning resolution

Today, many people think that a *4800 dpi* scanner must be better than a *2400* or *1200* or *300 dpi* scanner. After all, it's higher resolution, and it costs more. But that higher resolution costs more than cash — it costs hard drive space and the time your computer spends chugging along to create that scan. And most of the time, you don't even need or want a high-resolution image.

When you scan something at 2400 dpi, you're scanning 2,400 *dots per inch.* Your monitor uses a pixel to display each dot. And very few monitors can display more than 2,000 pixels across their entire screen. The result? When you scan something at 2400 dpi and view it on your screen, you're going to see a huge close-up of only about 1 inch of your image.

There's only one reason to scan at the highest resolution your scanner offers: when you're creating a file to be printed professionally or saved for relatives — old family photos, for example. After you've scanned the images, copy the huge files to a CD or DVD for safekeeping. Then delete the scans from your hard drive so they don't consume valuable space.

Most of the time, a much lower resolution will do the job, as shown in Table 7-1. In fact, for e-mail or Web sites, a lower resolution is better because these lean and mean files take up less space and load faster.

Table 7-1   General Guidelines for Scanner Settings

To Scan This . . .	For This . . .	Use This dpi Setting . . .	And Save As This
4-x-6-inch photo	E-mail	100	JPG
4-x-6-inch photo	Web	100	JPG
Anything	Printing	600	TIF
Letter	Faxing	200	TIF
Text	OCR*	300	TIF
Anything	Archive	2400	TIF

* OCR stands for optical character recognition — software that reads a scanned piece of text and converts it to letters and numbers for a word processor.

Use Table 7-1 as a general guideline; your scanner may not offer these exact resolutions. Try several scans at varying resolutions to see which looks best to you. Delete the ones that don't look nice, save the ones that do, and remember the setting you used for future reference.

Dealing with scans that look awful

Like nearly everything but eating, scanning requires practice. Okay, maybe eating Dungeness crab from the shell requires a bit of practice, but you get the point. Making practice scans doesn't cost you any money, so experiment with your scanning settings. You can always delete the scans that don't look quite right.

If you'll be scanning lots of things, consider buying some graphics software like Adobe Photoshop Elements. You'll be amazed at how much better a scanned photo looks when touched up.

But if it's just you, Windows Vista, and your scanner, these tips will help produce the best scans:

✔ Never clean your scanner with paper towels because they can leave tiny scratches on the glass. Instead, use standard glass cleaner and a lint-free rag, similar to the one packaged with some computer monitors. Spray the cleaner on the rag, not the glass itself.

✔ As with most computer parts, scanners rarely come packaged with their latest drivers. To update your scanner's drivers, visit the scanner manufacturer's Web site. Manufacturers constantly update a product's drivers to fix problems as they're discovered by disgruntled users like yourself.

✔ Before making your first scan, make sure that your monitor is displaying all the colors it can. Right-click a blank part of your desktop, choose Personalize and click Display Settings. Change the Colors setting to the highest available (32-bit, if possible).

Troubleshooting Your Scanner

Most manufacturers sell scanners in the "locked" position to keep their internal organs from being damaged during the trip from their factories to your desk. As soon as you unpack your scanner, look for its lock: a little round area with a small slot in the middle. Push a quarter into the slot and turn it toward the "unlocked" icon. If not unlocked, scanners make a horrid grinding noise instead of scanning.

Planning to move your scanner to another room? Be sure to lock it before moving it.

See whether Windows Vista recognizes it

See whether Windows Vista can even tell that your scanner's plugged in by following these steps:

1. **Choose Control Panel from the Start menu and click the Hardware and Sound category.**

2. **Choose the Scanners and Cameras icon (shown in the margin).**

   Look for icons for any scanners and cameras connected to your PC.

   If your scanner isn't listed, click the Refresh button. Still don't see it? Turn your scanner off, wait 30 seconds, turn it back on, and make sure that it's plugged into your PC. (As a last resort, try restarting your PC and then returning to this screen.)

3. **Click your scanner's icon and click the Properties button.**

   The Properties dialog box for your scanner appears.

4. **Click the Test Scanner button on the General tab.**

   Your PC makes a cursory check to make sure that the scanner's plugged in.

Let it warm up

Scanners not only take a few minutes to warm up, but they often need to warm up again when they haven't been used for a little while. If you see an error message when you try to scan something, wait a minute and try again. Your scanner may have needed that time to get back on its feet.

Chapter 8

Getting Online and in Touch

● ●

In This Chapter

▶ Exploring the Internet

▶ Using Windows Mail

▶ Thinking about security

● ●

*S*ome people consider an Internet connection to be optional, but Windows Vista prefers *mandatory*, thank you very much. Even when being installed, Windows Vista starts reaching for the Internet, eager for any hint of a connection. After checking in with the Internet, Windows Vista kindly nudges your computer's clock to the correct time. Some motives are less pure: Windows Vista checks with Microsoft to make sure that you're not installing a pirated copy.

This chapter explains how to connect with the Internet, visit Web sites, and find all the good stuff online. It also covers ways to keep out the bad stuff. The Internet is full of bad neighborhoods, and this chapter explains how to avoid viruses, spyware, hijackers, and other Internet parasites.

While Internet Explorer turns the Internet into a multimedia magazine, Windows Mail turns it into your personalized post office, where you never need fumble for a stamp. A Windows Vista freebie, Windows Mail lets you send letters and files to anybody in the world who has an e-mail account. (And that's just about everybody, these days.)

Cruising the Web

Today, most people take the Internet for granted, much like a telephone line. Instead of marveling at the Internet's internal gearing, they've grown accustomed to this new land called *cyberspace*, and its healthy stock of attractions.

Everybody needs four things to connect to the Web: a computer, Web browser software, a modem, and an Internet service provider (ISP).

You already have the computer, and Vista comes with a Web browser called Internet Explorer. Most PCs include a built-in modem. (If yours doesn't, you'll find out when you first try to set up your ISP.)

That means most people only need to find an ISP, and you can usually find one listed in your local Yellow Pages under *Computers — Online Services & Internet* or *Telecommunications.* Or ask your local computer dealer for names and numbers. And don't forget your telephone provider (who may offer DSL Internet service) or your cable television provider (who may offer cable Internet service).

Although television signals come wafting through the air to your TV set for free (unless you're paying for cable), you must pay an ISP for the privilege of surfing the Web. Specifically, you pay the ISP for a password and account name. When your computer's modem connects to your ISP's computers, Internet Explorer automatically enters your password and account name, and you're ready to surf the Web.

All browsers work basically the same way. Every Web page comes with a specific address, just like houses do. Internet Explorer lets you move between pages in three different ways:

✔ By pointing and clicking a button or link that automatically whisks you away to another page

✔ By typing a sometimes complicated string of code words (the Web address) into the Address box of the Web browser and pressing Enter

✔ By clicking the navigation buttons on the browser's toolbar, which is usually at the top of the screen (see Table 8-1)

The first way is the easiest. However, Web page designers get mighty creative these days; without the little hand pointer, it's often hard to tell where to point and click. Some buttons look like standard elevator buttons; others can look like fuzzy dice or tiny vegetables. But when you click a button, the browser takes you to the page relating to that button. Clicking the fuzzy dice may bring up a betting-odds sheet for local casinos, for example, and vegetables may bring information about the local Farmer's Market.

Hover your mouse pointer over a confusing Internet Explorer button to see its purpose in life.

Table 8-1 Navigating with Internet Explorer's Buttons

This Button	*. . . Is Called This . . .*	*. . . and Does This*
←	Back	Pointed and clicked yourself into a dead end? Click the Back button to head for the last Web page you visited. If you click the Back button enough times, you wind up back at your home page, where you began.
→	Forward	After you click the Back button, you can click Forward to revisit a page.

(continued)

Table 8-1 *(continued)*

This Button	*. . . Is Called This . . .*	*. . . and Does This*
	Favorites Center	Clicking the yellow star — the Favorites Center button — reveals the Favorites Center, a list of links leading to your favorite Web sites.
	Add to Favorites	Click this yellow plus sign to add your currently viewed Web page to your Favorites list.
	Home	If you get stuck as you explore the Internet, click the Home button along the top to move back into familiar territory. (Click the arrow to its right if you want to change your Home page.)
	RSS Feed	When this gray button appears orange, you know the site offers Really Simple Syndication, a quick way to read the site's headlines without actually visiting.
	Print	Click here to print the Web site as you see it. (Click the tiny arrow to its right for printing options, including the capability to see a preview.)
	Page	These options relate to the current page: Enlarging its text size, for example, or saving it as a file.

This Button	... Is Called This ...	... and Does This
	Tools	This opens a menu full of Internet Explorer tweaks, letting you make adjustments to the pop-up blocker and phishing filter, among others.

Sending E-Mail

If you've used Outlook Express, Windows XP's bundled e-mail program, you'll feel right at home with Windows Mail. Both programs are basically the same, with almost identical menus. Windows Mail can import all your old Outlook Express accounts, contacts, and e-mail. If you upgrade to Vista on your Windows XP system, Windows Mail is even smart enough to import your information automatically.

The Windows Mail screen, shown in Figure 8-1, splits your e-mail into two columns: The Folders side, along the left, automatically stores and sorts your e-mail. The work screen, along the right, lets you see and tinker with your e-mail.

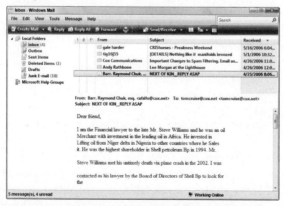

Figure 8-1: On the left, Windows Mail displays your folders; the selected folder's contents spill out to the top right, and the preview of the highlighted mail appears in the bottom right.

The folders in Windows Mail work much like traditional in baskets and out baskets for sorting memos. Click any folder's name to peek inside, and you're in for a pleasant surprise. Unlike your own office, Windows Mail automatically sorts your information into the following folders:

- **Inbox:** When you connect to the Internet, Windows Mail grabs any waiting e-mail and places it in your Inbox folder. On PCs with a broadband Internet connection, Windows Mail checks for new mail every 30 minutes — or whenever you click the Send/Receive button on the toolbar.

  Reduce your 30-minute wait by choosing Options from the Tools menu, clicking the General tab, and changing the number of minutes in the Check for New Messages Every X Minutes box.)

- **Outbox:** When you send or reply to a message, Windows Mail immediately tries to connect to the Internet and send it. If you're already connected, Windows Mail immediately fires it off to its recipient.

- **Sent Items:** *Every* piece of e-mail you've sent lingers in here, leaving a permanent record. (To kill the particularly embarrassing ones, right-click them and choose Delete.)

- **Deleted Items:** The Deleted Items folder serves as Windows Mail's Recycle Bin, letting you retrieve accidental deletions. To delete something permanently from the Deleted Items folder, right-click it and choose Delete from the pop-up menu.

  To keep deleted mail from cluttering your Deleted Items folder, choose Options from the Tools menu, click the Advanced Tab, and click the Maintenance button. From there, select the Empty Messages from the 'Deleted Items' Folder on Exit check box. If you'd prefer to clear out this folder when *you* choose to do so, click Edit from the main menu and choose Empty 'Deleted Items' Folder.

- **Drafts:** When you're midway through writing an e-mail and want to finish it later, choose Save from your e-mail's File menu. The letter moves to your Drafts folder until you're ready to revive it.

- **Junk E-mail:** Windows Mail sniffs out potential junk mail and drops suspects into this folder.

Exactly what do I need to send and receive e-mail?

To send e-mail to friend or foe with Windows Mail, you need three things:

✔ **An e-mail account:** The next section describes how to set up Windows Mail to work with your e-mail account. Most ISPs give you a free e-mail address along with your Internet access.

✔ **The e-mail address for your friend or foe:** Locate your friends' e-mail addresses by simply asking them. An address consists of a *user name* (which occasionally resembles the user's real name), followed by the @ sign, followed by the name of your friend's Internet service provider. The e-mail address of an America Online user with the user name Jeff9435 would be `jeff9435@aol.com`. (Unlike your local post office, e-mail doesn't tolerate any spelling errors. Precision is a must.)

✔ **Your message:** Here's where the fun finally starts: typing your letter. After you type the person's e-mail address and your message, press the Send button. Windows Mail routes your message in the right direction.

You can find people's e-mail addresses on business cards, Web sites, and even return addresses. Whenever you reply to e-mail, Windows Mail automatically adds that person's e-mail address to your list of contacts.

If you misspell part of an e-mail address, your sent message will bounce back to your own Inbox, with a confusing *undeliverable* message attached. Check the spelling of the address and try again. If it bounces again, humble yourself: Pick up the phone and ask the person if you have the right address.

To see the contents of any folder, click it. That folder's contents spill out to the top right. Click any mail, and its contents appear in the Preview pane beneath.

Setting up your e-mail account

In order to send or receive e-mail in Windows Mail, you need these three things, all available from your ISP: your user name, your password, and a working Internet connection. (You've already used these things if you successfully set up your Internet account.)

Most people set up more than one e-mail address, as well as the free account from their ISP. Whether you're setting up your 1st or your 40th e-mail account, follow these six steps:

1. **Set up your Internet account and open Windows Mail.**

   You need to set up your Internet account *first,* or your e-mail won't have any way to reach the Internet.

    To call up Windows Mail for the first time, open the Start menu and click the Windows Mail icon (shown in the margin). If you don't see this icon, choose All Programs and then click Windows Mail. Windows Mail hops onto the screen, ready to be set up to send and receive your e-mail, as shown in Figure 8-2.

Figure 8-2: When loaded for the first time, Windows Mail offers to set up your e-mail account.

   If the screen in Figure 8-2 doesn't appear automatically, open Windows Mail and choose Accounts from the Tools menu. Click the Add button, choose E-mail Account, and click Next to bring up the window in Figure 8-2, ready to add an e-mail account.

2. **Type your name and click Next.**

   This name will appear in the From box of all your e-mail, so most people simply type in their own name, as shown in Figure 8-2. Names like *DragonSlayer* may come back to haunt you.

3. **Type your e-mail address and click Next.**

   This is your user name, the @ sign, and your ISP, all information that your ISP must provide you with. For example, if your user name is *jeff4265* and your ISP's name is *charternet.com,* then type **jeff4265@charternet. com** into the E-Mail Address box.

4. **Choose your server type and the names for your incoming and outgoing mail servers, and click Next.**

   Here, you need to know what *type* of e-mail account the service uses. It's a weird word like POP3, IMAP, or HTTP. Most ISPs send you these handy settings and instructions through the post office. If you've lost them, visit your ISP's Web site or call your ISP's tech support folks and ask them for their mail server's *name* and *type*. Table 8-2 lists the information required by some common e-mail services.

   Google's Gmail, AOL, and Yahoo! all require you to click the box marked My Server Requires Authentication on this page.

Table 8-2   E-Mail Settings for Popular ISPs

Service	E-Mail Type	Incoming Mail Server	Outgoing Mail Server
Google Gmail (See the related sidebar for additional settings that Gmail accounts need.)	POP3	pop.gmail. com	smtp.gmail. com
America Online (AOL) (See the related sidebar for additional settings that AOL accounts need.)	IMAP	imap.aol. com	smtp.aol. com
Yahoo! (Only paid Yahoo! e-mail accounts can receive mail through Windows Mail.)	POP3	pop.mail. yahoo	smtp.mail. yahoo

5. **Type your account name and password and click Next.**

Finishing up your AOL account in Windows Mail

Even after finishing Steps 1 through 6 to set up your AOL account in Windows Mail, your account won't work correctly until you jump through the following hoops:

1. **Choose Accounts from Windows Mail's Tools menu to see your e-mail account (or accounts).**

2. **Select the AOL account you created, choose Properties, and click the Servers tab.**

3. **Click the My Server Requires Authentication check box and click Apply.**

4. **Click the Advanced tab.**

5. **In the Outgoing Mail (SMTP) box, change the number to 587 and click Apply.**

6. **Click the IMAP tab and click to remove the check from the Store Special Folders on IMAP Server box.**

7. **Click Apply, click OK, and click Close.**

If a message asks you to download folders from the mail server, click Yes.

For your account name, enter the part of your e-mail address before the @ sign. Then type the password for that account. Check the Remember Password box to fetch your mail automatically in the background.

Check the Secure Password Authentication box *only* if your Internet provider requests it. (Yahoo does, for example.)

6. **Click Finish.**

That's it. You should now be able to send and receive e-mail on Windows Mail.

Here are some other handy hints for working with Windows Mail:

✔ If the settings don't work or don't look right, they're easy to change. Choose Accounts from the Tools menu and double-click the name of the account that needs tweaking. These steps also let you change the way Windows Mail lists your account's name, perhaps changing the obtuse *pop.mail.yahoo* to plain old *Yahoo*, for example.

Finishing up your Gmail account in Windows Mail

After you set up your Gmail account, you need to jump through a few extra hoops before it works with Windows Mail:

1. **Choose Accounts from Windows Mail's Tools menu to see your e-mail account (or accounts).**

2. **Select the Gmail account you created, choose Properties, and click the Servers tab.**

3. **Click the My Server Requires Authentication check box and click Apply.**

4. **Click the Advanced tab.**

5. **Check the box next to This Server Requires a Secure Connection (SSL) under Outgoing Mail (SMTP).**

    The Incoming Mail port changes to 995.

6. **Enter 465 in the Outgoing mail (SMTP) field.**

7. **Click Apply, click OK, and click Close.**

✔ Some ISPs let you create up to five different e-mail accounts. Feel free to create a "disposable" e-mail account to use when you sign up for online offers or fill out temporary forms. When that account becomes plagued with spam, simply delete it and create a new one.

✔ Be sure to make your favorite e-mail account your *default* account — the one listed as the return address on every e-mail you send. To set your default account, choose Accounts from the Tools menu, click your most often used account, and click the Set as Default button.

✔ Back up these settings to avoid the hassle of ever filling them out again: Choose Accounts from the Tools menu and click your account's name. Then click the Export button to save your account information as an IAF (Internet Account File), a format that works with most other mail programs. To import these settings back into mail — or into your laptop's mail program — choose Accounts on the Tools menu and then select Import.

Composing and sending an e-mail

Ready to send your first e-mail? After you've set up Windows Mail with your e-mail account, follow these steps to compose your letter and drop it in the electronic mailbox, sending it through virtual space to the recipient's computer:

1. **Open Windows Mail and click the Create Mail icon from the program's menu.**

If you don't see a Create Mail icon along the top (it looks like the one in the margin), click the File menu, select New, and choose Mail Message.

A New Message window appears, as shown in Figure 8-3.

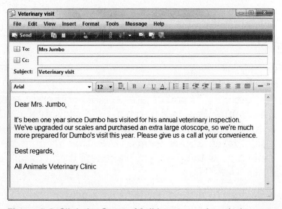

Figure 8-3: Click the Create Mail button, and a window appears for you to compose and send e-mail.

If you've set up more than one account, as described in the previous section, Windows Mail automatically addresses the mail with your *default* account — usually the first e-mail account you create in Windows Mail. To send your mail from one of your other e-mail accounts, should you have one, click the downward-pointing arrow in the From box — the box currently listing your e-mail address — and select your other account.

To send a quick e-mail to somebody in your Contacts folder, right-click his or her name, choose Action, and select Send E-mail. Windows Mail opens an e-mail already addressed to that person, saving you a step.

2. Type your friend's e-mail address into the To box.

Type the person's e-mail address into the To box. Or, click the To button (shown in the margin) next to where you type an address: A window appears, listing the names of people listed in your Contacts folder. Click your friend's name, click the To button, and click OK.

Sending or forwarding a message to several people? Preserve their privacy by clicking the Bcc button (shown in the margin) instead of the To button. That still sends them the same message but hides their e-mail addresses from each other, preserving their privacy. (If your Bcc button is missing, reveal it by clicking an e-mail's View menu and choosing All Headers.)

To let *everybody* see each other's e-mail addresses, select their names and click the Cc button, shown in the margin. (Unless the recipients all know each other, this is considered bad etiquette.)

3. Fill in the Subject box.

Although optional, the Subject line lets your friends know why you're bugging them. That makes it easier for your friends to sort their mail.

4. Type your message into the large box at the bottom of the window.

Type whatever you want and for as long as you want. There's very little limit on the size of a text file.

5. Want to attach a file to your message? Drag and drop the file onto the message. Or click the paper clip icon, navigate to the file, and double-click the file's name to attach it.

Most ISPs balk at sending files larger than about 5MB, however, which rules out most MP3 files and some digital photos.

6. **Click the Send button in the box's top-left corner.**

   Whoosh! Windows Mail dials your modem, if necessary, and whisks your message through the Internet
   pipelines to your friend's mailbox. Depending on the
   speed of the Internet connection, mail arrives anywhere within 15 seconds to five days, with a few minutes being the average.

   No Send button? Then click File in the New Message
   window and choose Send Message.

Reading a received e-mail

If you keep Windows Mail running while you're connected to
the Internet, you'll know when a new letter arrives. Your computer makes a little hiccup to herald its arrival. You'll also
spot a tiny Windows Mail icon in your desktop's bottom-right
corner, right next to the clock.

To check for any new mail when Windows Mail isn't running,
load the program from the Start menu. When it loads, click the
Send/Receive button (or click the Tools menu, choose Send
and Receive and then choose Send and Receive All). Windows
Mail logs on to the Internet, sends any outgoing mail you have
sitting around, and grabs any incoming mail to place in your
Inbox.

Follow these steps to read the letters in your Inbox and either
respond or file them away into one of the program's many
folders:

1. **Open Windows Mail and look at your Inbox.**

   Depending on how Windows Mail is set up, you can
   do this step in several different ways. If you see an
   opening screen announcing that you have unread mail
   in your Inbox, click the words Unread Mail to start
   reading. Or, if you see folders along the left side of
   Windows Mail, click the word Inbox.

   Either way, Windows Mail shows you the messages in
   your Inbox, and they look something like Figure 8-4.
   Each subject is listed, one by one, with the newest
   one at the top.

Figure 8-4: Click the word Inbox in Windows Mail to see your newly received messages.

Want your newest e-mails to appear at the list's *bottom?* Then click the word Received at the top of the Received column. Windows Mail re-sorts everything, but now places your newest message at the bottom. (You can also sort mail by subject or the sender's name by clicking those column headers.)

Folders with messages you *haven't* read appear in boldface type, like the Inbox, Deleted Items, and Drafts folders in Figure 8-4. Once you've read all the messages in a folder, the folder's name turns back to normal.

2. **Click the subject column on any message to read it.**

Click any message, and Windows Mail spills that message's contents into the screen's bottom portion, as shown in Figure 8-5, ready for you to read. To see the entire message in its own window, double-click it.

3. **From here, Windows Mail leaves you with several options, each described in the following list:**

   - **You can do nothing.** The message simply sets up camp in your Inbox folder until you delete it.

   - **You can respond to the message.** Click the Reply icon along the top of Windows Mail (or choose Reply to Sender from the Message menu), and a new window appears, ready for you to type your response. The window is just like the one that appears when you first compose a message but with a handy difference: This window is pread-dressed with the recipient's name and the sub-ject. Also, the original message details (including the actual message itself) may appear at the bottom of the message area.

- **You can file the message.** Right-click the mes-sage and choose either Move to Folder or Copy to Folder; then select the desired folder from the resulting dialog box and click OK. Or drag and drop the message to the desired folder along the left side of your screen.

- **You can print the message.** Click the Print icon along the menu's top, and Windows Mail shoots your message to the printer to make a paper copy.

- **You can delete the message.** Click the Delete button to toss the message into your Deleted Items folder. Your deleted messages sit inside the folder until you right-click the Deleted Items folder and choose Empty 'Deleted Items' Folder. For automatic deletion, choose Tools, select Options, click the Advanced tab, click Maintenance, and choose Empty Messages from the Deleted Items Folder on Exit.

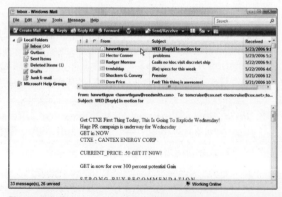

Figure 8-5: Click a message's subject line to see the message's contents.

Staying Safe Through It All

The Internet is not a safe place. Some people design Web sites specifically to exploit the latest Windows vulnerabilities — the ones Microsoft hasn't yet had time to patch. This section explains some of Internet Explorer's safety features, as well as other safe travel tips when navigating the Internet.

Avoiding evil add-ons and hijackers

Microsoft designed Internet Explorer to let programmers add extra features through *add-ons*. By installing an add-on program — toolbars, stock tickers, and program launchers, for example — people could wring a little more work out of Internet Explorer. Similarly, many sites use *ActiveX* — a fancy word for little programs that add animation and other flashy tricks to a Web site.

Unfortunately, dastardly programmers began creating add-ons and ActiveX programs that *harm* users. Some of these add-ons can spy on your activities, bombard your screen with additional ads, redirect your home page to another site, or make your modem dial long-distance numbers to porn sites. Worse yet, some renegade add-ons can install themselves as soon as you visit a Web site — without asking your permission.

Windows Vista packs several guns to combat these trouble-makers. First, if a site tries to sneak a program onto your computer, Internet Explorer quickly blocks it, sending a warning (shown in Figure 8-6) across the top of the Internet Explorer screen. Clicking the warning reveals your options, shown in Figure 8-7.

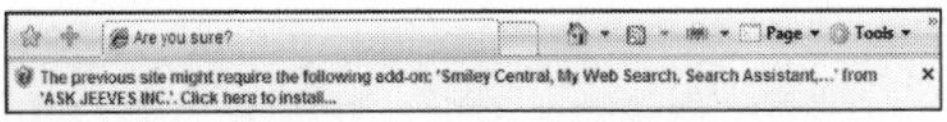

Figure 8-6: Internet Explorer blocks a program.

Figure 8-7: The warning strip shows your options.

Unfortunately, Internet Explorer can't tell the good downloads from the bad, leaving the burden of proof to you. But if you see a message like the one shown in Figure 8-6 and you *haven't* requested a download, chances are the site is trying to harm you: Don't download the program or install the ActiveX control.

If a bad add-on creeps in somehow, you're not completely out of luck. Internet Explorer's Add-on Manager lets you disable it. To see all the add-on programs installed in Internet Explorer (and remove any that you know are bad), follow these steps:

1. **Choose Manage Add-Ons from Internet Explorer's Tools menu and then choose Enable or Disable Add-ons from the pop-up menu.**

   Don't mistakenly choose Find More Add-ons. That takes you to Microsoft's store, which tries to sell you bushels of over-priced add-ons.

   The Manage Add-ons window appears, as shown in Figure 8-8, letting you see all currently or previously loaded add-ons, as well as add-ons running without permission. It also lets you see downloaded ActiveX controls, which often cause the most trouble.

2. **Click the Add-on that gives you trouble and choose Disable.**

   Click the Show drop-down box at the top of the Manage Add-ons Window to see the four types of add-ons. Choose another of these types to see add-ons listed for that category. If you spot the name of an unwanted toolbar or other bad program, here's your chance to purge it.

3. **Repeat the process for each unwanted add-on and then click the OK button.**

   You probably need to restart Internet Explorer for the change to take effect.

Figure 8-8: Internet Explorer's Manage Add-ons window lets you see all installed add-ons and remove the ones you don't like.

Not all add-ons are bad. Many good ones let you play movies, hear sounds, or view special content on a Web site. Don't delete an add-on simply because it's listed in the Add-on Manager.

Keep the following tips in mind when dealing with add-ons and the Add-on Manager:

✔ On the rare instance that disabling an add-on prevents a page from loading, click that add-on's name in Step 2 of the preceding steps and click the Enable button to return it to working order.

✔ Internet Explorer's Add-on Manager disables add-ons fairly easily; but if you spot a particularly evil one, remove it completely by clicking the Delete ActiveX button instead of the Disable button.

✔ How the heck do you tell the good add-ons from the bad? Unfortunately, there's no sure way of telling. The best way is to avoid being hijacked in the first place, mainly by not installing things Internet Explorer has tried to block.

> ✔ Make sure that Internet Explorer's defenses are up: Choose Pop-Up Blocker from its Tools menu. If you see Turn Off Pop-Up Blocker in the pop-up menu, you're all set. Otherwise, if you see Turn On Pop-Up Blocker, the feature is turned off. Select this command to turn it back on.

Stopping pop-up ads

Internet Explorer's pop-up blocker filters out most pop-ups, sparing you from wading through an annoying flurry of pop-up advertisements. Expect a few to still creep through, however, as it's not perfect.

Some sites rely on pop-ups as part of their design — click a product, and a small pop-up gives you more information, for example. If you encounter a site that doesn't work correctly unless you can see the pop-ups, you can easily turn the pop-ups back on. Click the message bar that appears across the top of Internet Explorer when a pop-up is blocked, and the following settings appear:

> ✔ **Temporarily Allow Pop-Ups:** Quick and convenient, this option lets you see the site's pop-ups during your current visit.

> ✔ **Always Allow Pop-Ups from This Site:** More dangerous, this places the site on your Allow Pop-ups list, letting it fling pop-ups without restriction. Only choose this setting for sites you trust, or you may be opening yourself to a deluge.

> ✔ **Settings:** This option lets you change how Internet Explorer handles pop-ups, even letting you turn off the pop-off blocker if you're one of the three people who enjoy them. You can also turn off Internet Explorer's notice that it's blocked a pop-up. The last option, More Settings, lets you further customize the pop-up blockers through the Pop-Up Blocker Settings page.

To stop Internet Explorer from making that little bubble-popping noise when it blocks a pop-up, choose Pop-Up Blocker from Internet Explorer's Tools menu. Select Pop-Up Blocker

Settings and remove the check mark from the Play a Sound When a Pop-Up Is Blocked box.

If Internet Explorer keeps throwing pop-ups your way, your pop-up blocker may be turned off. To turn it back on, choose Pop-Up Blocker from Internet Explorer's Tools menu and choose Turn On Pop-Up Blocker.

Pop-up blocker still not working? Then your PC may be infected with spyware, as that's a main symptom. I describe spyware and its removal later in this chapter.

Buying from secure Web sites

Whenever you buy something from a Web site, make sure that you're typing in your credit card number onto a *secure* Web site. How can you tell if a site's secure?

In Internet Explorer, look for a little lock next to the site's link in the Address bar. Click the lock icon to see the site's security certificate. Make sure that the current Web site's name is actually listed in the Issued To area and that the dates listed on the Valid From area are still valid.

If the site looks suspicious, don't enter your credit card number. Instead, shop from a different site. Or simply call the company on the phone and place your order by phone. (You usually find phone numbers by clicking the words Contact Us on the site's home page.)

Here's an easy way to remember the different colors displayed in Internet Explorer's Address bars: yellow means *slow down*, as that site is suspected of phishing, described in the next section. Red means *stop*, as you're viewing a known phishing site.

Avoiding phishing scams

Eventually, you'll receive an e-mail from your bank, eBay, PayPal, or a similar Web site announcing a problem with your account. Invariably, the e-mail offers a handy link to click, saying you must enter your user name and password to set things in order.

Don't do it, no matter how realistic the e-mail and Web site may appear. You're seeing an ugly industry called *phishing*. Fraudsters send out millions of these messages worldwide, hoping to convince a few frightened souls into typing their precious account names and passwords.

How do you tell the real e-mails from the fake ones? It's easy, actually, because *all* these e-mails are fake. Finance-related sites never, ever e-mail you a link for you to click on and enter your password. If you're suspicious, visit the company's *real* Web site — by typing the Web address by hand. Then look for their security area and forward the e-mail, asking whether it's legitimate. Chances are, it's not.

Vista's new version of Internet Explorer employs four safe-guards to thwart phishing scams:

- ✔ Windows Mail warns you with a message when it spots a suspicious e-mail heading for your Inbox. Click the message's Delete button if the mail is bogus. Click Unblock on the rare chance that Vista mistakenly blocked a legitimate e-mail.

- ✔ When you first run Internet Explorer, the program offers to turn on its Phishing Filter. Take Internet Explorer up on its offer. Unlike many of Vista's safety features, the Phishing Filter provides a very non-obtrusive safety net.

- ✔ Internet Explorer examines every Web page for suspicious signals. If a site seems suspicious, Internet Explorer's Address bar — the normally white area that lists the Web site's address — turns yellow. Internet Explorer sends a pop-up warning that you're viewing a suspected phishing site.

- ✔ Internet Explorer compares a Web site's address with a list of known phishing sites. If it finds a match, the Phishing Filter keeps you from entering, shown in Figure 8-9. Should you ever spot that screen, close the Web page.

If you've already entered your name and password into a phishing site, take action immediately. Visit the *real* Web site and change your password. Change your username, too, if possible. Then contact the bank or company and ask them for help. They may be able to stop the thieves before they wrap their electronic fingers around your funds.

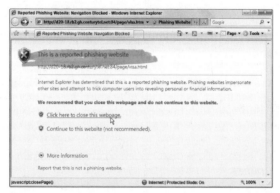

Figure 8-9: Internet Explorer detects many phishing sites and warns you from entering.

Removing spyware and parasites

Spyware and *parasites* are programs that latch onto Internet Explorer without your knowledge. The sneakiest programs may try to change your home page, dial toll numbers with your modem, and spy on your Web activity — sneaking your surfing habits back to the spyware program's publisher.

Most spyware programs freely admit to being spies — usually on the 43rd page of the 44-page agreement you're supposed to read before installing the program.

Nobody wants these ugly programs, of course, so they do tricky things to keep you from removing them. That's where Vista's new Windows Defender program comes in. It stops some spyware from installing itself automatically and pries off spyware that has already latched onto your PC. Best yet, Windows Update keeps Windows Defender up-to-date to recognize and destroy the latest strains of spyware.

To make sure that Windows Defender is running automatically on your PC, visit Windows Security Center. When running automatically, Windows Defender scans your PC automatically each evening and alerts you to any newfound spyware.

To make Windows Defender scan your PC immediately, a potential solution when your PC is acting strange, click the Start menu, choose All Programs, and launch Windows Defender. Click the Scan button and wait for it to finish.

Several other anti-spyware programs can also scan your computer for spyware, carefully snipping out any pieces that they find. Some of these programs are free in the hopes that you'll buy the more full-featured version later. Ad-Aware (www.lavasoftusa.com) and Spybot Search & Destroy (www.safer-networking.org) are two of the most popular programs.

Don't be afraid to run more than one spyware scanner on your PC. Each does its own scan, killing off any spyware it finds.

Parental controls

A feature much welcomed by parents and much booed by their children, Vista's Parental Controls, offers several new ways to police how people can access the computer, as well as the Internet. In fact, people who share their PCs with room-mates may welcome the Parental Controls as well.

The Parental Controls let you dictate what a person can and can't do on the Internet. They also keep tabs on how the person is using the PC, sending you reports on exactly when they're using it, what Web sites they're visiting, and what programs they're using.

To set Parental Controls, you must own an Administrator account. If everybody shares one PC, make sure that the kids have Limited accounts. If your children have their own PCs, create an Administrator account on their PCs for yourself and change their accounts to Limited.

To set up Vista's Parental Controls, follow these steps:

1. **Click the Start button, choose Control Panel, and then choose Set Up Parental Controls in the User Accounts and Family Safety section.**

   If Vista's built-in policeman says, "A program needs your permission to continue," feel free to click the Continue button.

2. **Click the user account you want to restrict.**

   Vista lets you add Parental Controls to only _one_ user account at a time, a process which caused considerable grief for Mr. and Mrs. Brady.

   When you choose a user account, the Parental Controls screen appears. The next steps take you through each section of the controls.

3. **Turn the Parental Controls on or off.**

   The Parental Controls area first presents two switches, letting you turn monitoring on or off.

   Parental Controls: This toggle switch simply turns on or off any restrictions you've set. It's a handy way to turn on the restrictions when your suspicions are aroused, or turn them off when they're not needed.

   Activity Reporting: This switch toggles Vista's activity reporting, which is where the PC spies on your children's habits, tells you exactly when they've logged on and off, what programs they've used or tried to use, and what Web sites they've visited or tried to visit.

4. **Set the Windows Vista Web Filter to determine what parts of the Web your child may visit.**

   Choosing this setting fetches a detailed page where you may pick and choose the parts of the Internet your child may view. You can add a few Web sites to the _blocked_ list, a handy way to punish your child by keeping her off MySpace.com for one week, for example. For ultimate control, block _every_ Web site, only adding safe ones to the _allowed_ list as needed.

   The Filter Web Content area lets you place checkmarks next to specific categories you'd like blocked from your child's view: pornography, gambling, Web chat, sex education, and similar topics. Be aware, however, that Web filters aren't 100 percent accurate; some unwanted sites will always slip through the cracks.

5. **Choose whether to allow file downloads and then click OK.**

   The final box at the bottom of this page lets you stop your child from downloading files, an easy way to keep them from downloading and installing programs without your knowledge. However, checking this box may also keep them from downloading files needed for schoolwork.

   Clicking OK returns you to the Parental Controls opening screen.

6. **Add restrictions on time limits, games, and specific programs and then set activity reports, clicking OK after each.**

   This huge category lets you block specific things on your PC rather than on the Internet:

   • **Time limits:** This option brings up a grid, letting you click on the hours when your child should be restricted from using the PC. Here's where you can make the PC off-limits after bed time, for example.

   • **Games:** You may allow or ban all games here, restrict access to games with certain ratings (ratings appear on most software boxes), and block or allow specific games.

   • **Allow and Block Specific Programs:** Here's where you can keep the kids out of your checkbook program, as well as particular games. You can block all programs, only allowing access to a few. Or, you can allow access to all but a few programs.

   • **Activity Reports:** This setting lists the activity of every user account on your PC. You can view lists of everybody's visited Web sites, downloaded files, log on and off times, played games, newly added contacts, Web Cam usage, accessed songs and videos, and much, much more. A handy summary on the first page sorts this vast amount of information into Top Ten lists for easy viewing.

Be sure to click Notifications, in the left pane of the Parental Controls area (on the initial Parental Controls screen). It sends you a reminder to view the activity reports of your children. You can set it to weekly, biweekly, monthly or never — an option that simply disables the notifications.

This page also lets you toggle a little icon that appears on your children's taskbar near their clock. Normally turned on, this lets your children know that you're spying on them — something you may not want them to know.

Chapter 9

Revving Up Office 2007

* * *

In This Chapter

▶ Understanding the system requirements

▶ Figuring out which Office 2007 Suite is right for you

▶ Introducing the new Office 2007 user interface

▶ Taking a look at the core Office 2007 applications

* * *

*Y*ou may be wondering what you can expect from the next generation of Microsoft Office. Well, you've come to the right place. *Microsoft Office 2007* is now in the works and soon to be released. This version includes significant enhancements to the overall look and feel of each application. You can call it a major facelift. The updated interface provides a cleaner, more streamlined appearance that is designed to make it easier for you to find the commands and features you need — when you need them. This streamlined look should enable you to produce effective documents even faster than before.

This chapter helps you get up to speed with the sweeping changes coming your way in Office 2007. Here, you read about the new and improved user interface for the core applications — Word, Excel, PowerPoint, Access, and Outlook. (Chapter 11 covers some new ways of doing old, familiar tasks in Microsoft Office 2007.)

Still plan to use Windows XP for awhile? Not a problem. You'll still be able to run Office 2007 as you ponder whether to upgrade to Windows Vista.

Will My Computer Run Office 2007?

According to Microsoft, you probably won't need to upgrade your hardware if you plan to upgrade from Office 2003 (the most recent version) to Office 2007. However, if you're using an earlier version of Microsoft Office (such as Office XP or Office 2000), you should ensure that you have the proper hardware before installing Office 2007.

Here's what you'll need:

- ✔ **Operating system:** Microsoft Windows XP (Service Pack 2) or later ("later" includes Windows Vista), or Microsoft Windows Server 2003 (or higher)

- ✔ **Hard drive:** 2GB required for installation; less storage space may actually be used, depending on which applications and programs you choose to install

- ✔ **Computer and processor:** 500 MHz processor or higher; 256MB RAM or higher; DVD drive (that's right — a plain old CD drive won't suffice!)

- ✔ **Monitor resolution:** Minimum 800 x 600; 1,024 x 768 or higher recommended

- ✔ **Internet connection:** Broadband connection — 128 Kbps or greater (for download and activation of products)

As of this writing, Microsoft has not yet released the "official" final system requirements for Microsoft Office 2007. However, the information included here should give you a general idea of what you'll likely need.

Which Suite Is Right for Me?

Microsoft Office consists of an integrated collection of full-featured applications that can greatly simplify your computing. Depending on your computing needs and the size of your wallet, you have a choice to make — which Microsoft Office 2007 Suite is right for you? Of course, if you work in an office, this choice may have already been made *for* you. If that's the case, lucky you! Feel free to hop on over to the next section and skip the gory details that follow.

Here are your options for the retail versions of Microsoft Office 2007:

- ✔ **Microsoft Office Home and Student 2007:** Includes Word (word processor), Excel (spreadsheet), PowerPoint (presentation graphics), and OneNote (information sharing)

- ✔ **Microsoft Office Standard 2007:** Includes Word, Excel, Outlook (communications), and PowerPoint

- ✔ **Microsoft Office Small Business 2007:** Includes Word, Excel, Outlook with Business Contact Manager, PowerPoint, and Publisher (desktop publishing)

- ✔ **Microsoft Office Professional 2007:** Includes Word, Excel, Outlook with Business Contact Manager, PowerPoint, Publisher, and Access (database)

Other suite offerings will be available only through OEMs (Microsoft Office Basic 2007) or volume licensing (Microsoft Office Professional Plus 2007 and Microsoft Office Enterprise 2007).

A Peek at the New "Look"

The most significant change to the new look of the core Microsoft Office 2007 applications is the ribbon that appears at the top of the screen (see Figure 9-1). The ribbon displays the most commonly used commands — formerly found on a complex maze of menus and dozens of toolbars in previous versions of Office. This setup makes it easier to find just what you're looking for as you're preparing your document.

Click the *Microsoft Office button* — that round Windows icon in the upper left corner of the application window — to access the File commands. You'll also notice a few of your favorite commands in the *Quick Access toolbar*, which appears just to the right of the Microsoft Office button. For starters, you see the Save, Undo, Redo/Repeat, and Print buttons. You can customize this toolbar to your heart's content if you want additional commands to always be available.

Microsoft Office button

Quick Access toolbar

Page Layout tab

Help icon

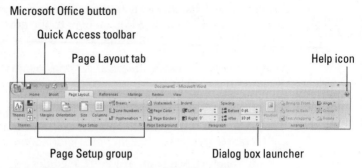

Page Setup group

Dialog box launcher

Figure 9-1: The Page Layout tab of the Word ribbon.

The ribbon consists of three different parts:

✔ **Tabs:** These tabs appear along the top of the ribbon and may vary in number, depending on which application you're working with and what you're doing in that application. The Home tab is where you find the most commonly used commands. Click another descriptive tab name to see the options contained there. If you're preparing to print a Word document, for example, click the Page Layout tab so that you can easily set up the document for printing.

✔ **Groups:** Each tab contains multiple groups of related items. The group names display at the bottom of each group. The Page Layout tab in Word, for example, has these groups: Themes, Page Setup, Page Background, Paragraph, and Arrange (as shown in Figure 9-1). Some groups have a little arrow icon in the bottom right corner, called a dialog box launcher, which opens a dialog box with commands related to that group.

✔ **Commands:** Within each group are related commands — buttons, boxes, menus, and so on. Some commands result in an immediate action, while others display a menu, dialog box, or drop-down pane.

Microsoft has done extensive research based on users' experiences to determine which commands should be placed where so that you can quickly and easily find what you need. Expect a bit of a learning curve, however, as you're getting used to this newfangled method of organization!

Want to focus on your document and use as much screen space as possible without the ribbon getting in your way? Just double-click the active tab on the ribbon. The tabs remain on-screen, but the commands are gone. They're only hiding, though. To display the ribbon again in all its glory, just click any of the ribbon tabs. The Ctrl+F1 keyboard shortcut also works as a toggle to hide and redisplay the ribbon.

The remaining sections in this chapter provide more details on other new features in the individual Office 2007 applications, along with figures that show you what's what.

What's in a Word?

Microsoft Word is the ubiquitous document authoring application included in all versions of Microsoft Office. With Word, you can create letters, reports, brochures, mailing labels, envelopes, and just about any other type of document you can imagine.

Here are some new features you'll have fun with in Word 2007:

✔ **Live preview:** This feature enables you to preview formatting changes — such as fonts, tables, styles, and templates — before you apply them to the document. Just select the text to affect and then point to the formatting commands in the ribbon. When you like what you see, select that command or option to immediately apply it to the document.

✔ **Mini toolbar:** When you select text in a document that you want to format and then point to the selection, you'll see a Mini toolbar pop up right next to the selection. Point to the Mini toolbar and click the desired option (see Figure 9-2).

✔ **Improved themes:** Word 2007 provides a much greater selection of themes, colors, fonts, and effects than previous versions. You find these options in the Themes group on the Page Layout tab.

✔ **Quick Styles:** On the Home tab, in the Styles group, you find many additional built-in styles that you can use to quickly apply multiple formats. Select the text and click the desired style button. To see additional styles, click the More down arrow to the right of the displayed styles.

Quick Styles

Mini toolbar

Selected text

Figure 9-2: Use the Mini toolbar to quickly apply formats to selected text in Word.

You Want to Excel!

Microsoft Excel is the spreadsheet component of Microsoft Office — the dependable number-cruncher that you've come to rely on when preparing anything from a simple table of information to budgets and more complex analyses.

Here are just a few of the new features in Excel 2007:

> ✔ **More colors and styles:** You can access many more font and fill colors in Excel 2007 than in previous versions. These features are located in the Font group on the Home tab. Point to different colors to see a live preview in your worksheet and then select the desired color. You'll also notice other expanded formatting options, such as cell styles (see Figure 9-3).

✔ **Page Layout view:** This new view offers similar advantages to the Page Layout view in Word. Rulers appear at the top and left side of the worksheet, to help you adjust the margins. Click in the designated boxes in the top or bottom of a previewed page to easily add a header or footer. The column and row headings display in this view. Plus, you can add data directly to the worksheet — just click in the desired cell and type!

✔ **Wrap Text button:** Remember the days when you had to select a menu command and then choose an option in a dialog box whenever you wanted to display multiple lines in a cell? Well, no more! Excel 2007 includes a Wrap Text button in the Alignment group of the Home tab. One click, and that's that.

✔ **More rows and columns:** The number of rows and columns available in a worksheet has increased dramatically. Each worksheet now has 1,048,576 rows and 16,384 columns. I'm not sure what you'd want to do with more than a million worksheet rows, but they're there if you need them!

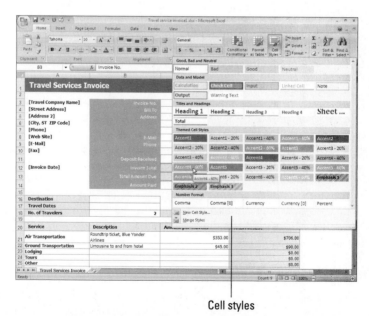

Cell styles

Figure 9-3: Excel 2007 offers many improved formatting enhancements.

You've Got the Power, Now What's Your Point?

Microsoft PowerPoint is the presentation graphics application that comes with most versions of Microsoft Office. With PowerPoint, you can create stunning presentations with a minimum of time and effort.

Keep an eye out for these cool new features in PowerPoint 2007:

- ✔ **Live preview:** With this feature, you can preview themes, animations, styles, and templates before you apply them to your presentation. Just select the text or object in the slide (if applicable) and then point to the commands in the ribbon to see a temporary preview on the slide. Select that command or option to immediately apply it to the slide(s).

- ✔ **New options for designing slide content:** The slide layouts in PowerPoint 2007 are more powerful than in previous editions. Some layouts offer placeholders that support either text or graphics (not just one or the other), which saves you time and gives you much more flexibility than the previous editions.

- ✔ **Picture tools:** When you select a picture in a slide (such as a photograph), you can apply special effects — such as glow, curved edges, or a reflection — to the picture's border.

- ✔ **SmartArt:** PowerPoint 2007 includes a plethora of new diagrams — called SmartArt — that relate to a process, hierarchy, cycle, or relationship (see Figure 9-4). You can even convert existing text, such as a bulleted list, into a diagram and edit diagram text in a text pane (rather than within the diagram itself).

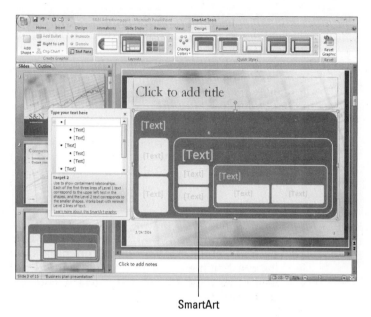

SmartArt

Figure 9-4: SmartArt provides many new diagramming tools for your PowerPoint presentations.

Access: The Cure for Chaotic Data

Microsoft Access is the full-featured database management program packaged with just a few versions of Microsoft Office. Access enables you to efficiently manage and organize large quantities of data and to prepare reports that summarize information based on that data.

You find these new or enhanced features in Access 2007:

✓ **Navigation pane:** The new Navigation pane provides a comprehensive look at the tables, queries, forms, and reports in a database. You also can create custom groups that show all the forms and reports associated with a particular table.

✔ **Prebuilt database solutions:** Access 2007 includes a new library of prebuilt database solutions that can get you started when creating a new database. You can use these files as a template that you can later tweak and enhance to meet your own needs.

✔ **Improved interface:** In addition to the Office 2007 user interface changes mentioned previously in this chapter, Access 2007 includes additional enhancements to the look and feel of the product (see Figure 9-5), including a tabbed windows view and improvements to the status bar, scroll bars, and title bar. Access 2007 more closely resembles Excel 2007, which should improve the ease of use.

✔ **Enhanced report features:** With Access 2007, you can save a variety of report views for different audiences and obtain real-time visual feedback. New filtering and sorting capabilities along with a grouping pane help you to further refine your reports and subsequently make better business decisions.

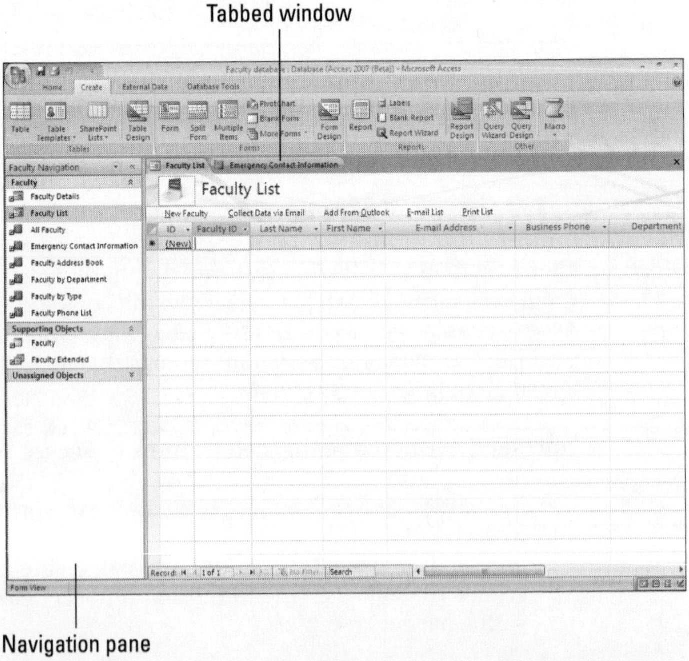

Tabbed window

Navigation pane

Figure 9-5: Access 2007 boasts many additional interface enhancements.

Here's Where to Improve Your Outlook

Microsoft Outlook is the personal information manager and communications program included in nearly all versions of Microsoft Office. With Outlook, you can send and receive e-mail, track appointments, keep a To Do list, maintain business and personal contact information, and much more.

Here are some of the new features that come with Outlook 2007:

- ✔ **To-Do bar:** A new To-Do bar can help you keep track of things to do, including upcoming calendar items (such as meetings, appointments, and events) and flagged messages and tasks. You can customize the To-Do bar to display only the information you need.

- ✔ **Preview files attached to messages:** Outlook 2007 enables you to see a preview of some types of file attachments directly in the Reading pane. When working with file attachments, *always* ensure that you have an up-to-date virus checker installed on your computer.

- ✔ **Assign names to color categories:** You can assign names to items that you categorize by color. This color coding applies to all items in Outlook, including messages, contacts, tasks, and calendar items, making it easier for you to find messages about a special project, for example, if you mark all messages related to that project with a single color category.

- ✔ **Enhanced search:** In Outlook 2007, you have more control over fine-tuning the search results so that you can find an important message even faster than before. You also can search for messages in multiple locations at once, rather than one measly folder at a time.

Part III
The Part of Tens

"How do you like that Aero glass interface on Vista? Nice, huh?"

In this part . . .

No *For Dummies* book would be complete without The Part of Tens section: Lists of ten easy-to-read informational nuggets. Of course, the lists don't always contain exactly ten, but you get the general idea.

Because this book is aimed at previewers — potential upgraders to Vista — the first list explains ten reasons why you may want to upgrade to Vista immediately, without waiting for it to come installed on a new PC.

Another list contains ten new ways to do old things with Microsoft's other big project: Office 2007. The last list provides ten ways to keep Vista (and your computer) running smoothly. Enjoy!

Chapter 10

Ten or So Reasons to Upgrade to Windows Vista

In This Chapter

▶ Thinking about searching and security

▶ Burning DVDs and more

*Y*ou'll see Windows Vista in the headlines quite a bit this year. The buzz starts in the technology section, ambles over to business columns, and eventually turns into news headlines. But amid all the buzz about Vista, there's one nagging question: Do you really *need* this thing?

This chapter describes some of the most tempting features Microsoft has worked into Vista, and what you'll find in them.

Improved Search

Windows XP really drags its feet when searching for files. Searching for a filename takes several minutes on a crowded hard drive, and if you're searching your files for a particular word or phrase, you're in for a long weekend. Vista, by contrast, spends its idle time fine-tuning an index of every word on your hard drive.

To keep that work handy, Vista places a Search box on the Start menu, atop every folder, and in a few other areas. The handy Search box and the up-to-date index make it faster than ever to find the files and programs you want.

Vista even updates its index with words on Web sites you've visited recently, letting you quickly call up that headline you remember reading last week.

Trying to find the right setting in the Control Panel's vast array of switches and options? As you type words describing that setting into the Control Panel's Search box — **firewall,** for example — Vista filters out every item that doesn't pertain to the firewall. Eventually, you'll only spot a few icons left, and they'll *all* pertain to your computer's firewall.

Security

Some may call it a nuisance, others call it User Account Protection, but Microsoft prefers to call it advanced security. Vista's built-in User Account Protection security not only keeps unwanted creatures from crawling into your PC, but it also stops the ones already inside your PC from *calling home* to their creators through the Internet. Whenever something in your PC tries to do something that could change Vista's settings, Vista asks for your permission.

Although all this security is indeed a bother, it's the only way to keep your PC and your files safe.

Even if you turn off the security features for your own account, leave them turned on for your kids' accounts or the account you create for your babysitter or housesitter. Vista security will keep them from mucking up your PC while you're away.

Windows Defender

Just about everybody's heard something about *spyware* — unwanted software that sneaks onto your PC. It then spies on your Web-browsing habits and sends the results to sneaky companies who fill your PC with ads targeted toward your interests.

But that's the least worrisome part of spyware. The big problem is that spyware makers don't create quality products. When something's wrong with your PC, spyware's the most likely suspect. Spyware-infested PCs experience slowdowns, conflicts with other software, and even crashes.

Vista's new Windows Defender seeks out and destroys spyware before it takes hold. Because companies constantly create new breeds of spyware, Microsoft automatically trains Windows Defender with Windows Update to recognize the latest spyware strains and pry them off your PC.

Parental Controls

Most parents don't let their children travel unknown neighborhoods without supervision. But what about the PC and its ticket to the Internet's chat rooms and adult Web sites? Vista's strict parental controls let parents control their kids' computer workouts by adding the following controls:

- ✔ Blocking specific Web sites and programs or blocking all but a few hand-picked Web sites and programs
- ✔ Filtering Web sites by their content
- ✔ Blocking file downloads
- ✔ Controlling the days or hours the PC is available
- ✔ Collecting detailed activity reports showing Web sites blocked/visited, programs run, games played, and instant messaging conversations held

Although Vista calls them *Parental* Controls, they let any administrator account holder control the activities of any standard account holder. That means you can finally control exactly how your roommates use your PC — if you let them use it at all.

And your boss can see exactly how much time you spend playing solitaire when you should be working. Be forewarned.

DVD Burning

Windows XP couldn't write to DVDs without the help of a third-party program. Vista can finally write to blank DVDs by itself, making DVDs an easy way to back up all those digital photos. Combine Vista's DVD Maker program with Vista's improved Movie Maker program, and you'll finally be able to burn your vacation videos to DVD and watch them in the living room.

Vista's built-in Backup program lets you automatically store your backed-up files to CDs *or* DVDs.

Runs on an Average PC

You may have heard how Vista won't run on older PCs, or it needs an expensive video card. But if your PC's running Windows XP, it will probably run Vista just fine.

As for the video card, Vista certainly looks its best when run on a PC with a high-powered video card. But it also looks fine on most PCs today. For proof, check out this book's color insert. One page shows Vista wearing its "high-powered video card" clothes. The next page shows how Vista looks on a PC with an average video card. The differences really aren't that obvious.

In fact, some people will turn off Vista's glass tabletop because all those reflections can be distracting.

Chapter 11

Ten New Ways of Doing Old Things in Microsoft Office 2007

*B*ecause of the significant changes to the user interface of the Microsoft Office applications, you may have trouble locating what you need as you're creating a document. The menu structure and toolbars that you were finally getting the hang of are now gone — replaced with a viable alternative, the *ribbon* — that should eventually save you much time and frustration.

The tricks listed here help you find your way through the unfamiliar Office 2007 jungle. Unless otherwise noted, each of these tips applies to all the core applications of Microsoft Office 2007.

 If you haven't read Chapter 9, you may want to do so before continuing here — that chapter illustrates the Office 2007 user interface and introduces some of the new or enhanced features.

Locating the File Commands

When you start one of the Office 2007 applications, you may wonder what happened to the trusty File menu. Well, you can access the File menu from the round Windows icon — the *Microsoft Office button* — located in the upper left corner of the application window. That's where you'll find the familiar commands that you know and love. Just click that icon to see the New, Open, Save, Save As, Print, and Close commands, among others. The Exit command appears as a button in the lower right corner of the File menu.

Some commands on the File menu include an arrow beside them. Point to the arrow to see additional options for that command. These options display in a pane to the right of the File commands. For example, point to the Save As arrow to see options for saving a file in an older format. Other options may be listed, depending on the application.

Finding Other Elusive Commands

Can't find the command you're looking for in the *ribbon* (that long horizontal bar of tabs, icons, and buttons at the top of the application)? Try any or all of these methods to locate the hidden command:

- ✔ First, try looking on another tab in the ribbon — the main tab that includes commonly used commands in an application is called the *Home tab*. Click other tabs to see additional options and commands related to the tab name.

- ✔ If that doesn't do the trick, try using a *dialog box launcher* — a little arrow icon in the bottom right corner of most groups within the ribbon.

  If you want to find commands related to character spacing in Word, for example, click the dialog box launcher in the Font group on the Home tab. The familiar Font dialog box displays, and you can find the options you want on the Character Spacing tab.

✔ Use the File menu to locate commands that were previously found via the Options command on the Tools menu in earlier versions of Microsoft Office. Click the Microsoft Office button and choose the Options button that appears at the bottom of the File menu (such as *Word Options* in Word, or *Excel Options* in Excel).

In the resulting dialog box, click an item in the left pane, such as Customization, to see options related to that item in the right pane. This dialog box is where you'll also find commands and program settings relating to AutoCorrect, save locations, add-ins, security and privacy settings, and more.

✔ Of course, you can always seek Help, if necessary. Press F1 or click the Help icon near the upper right corner of the application window. See "Getting Help When You Need It," later in this chapter, for more details.

Understanding the New File Formats

You may have heard that Office 2007 includes new XML (Extensible Markup Language) file formats that help keep your file sizes smaller and more secure. These files take advantage of the Microsoft Office Open XML Formats. It sounds complicated, but fear not — you don't need to understand XML.

You'll notice that some file extensions — those characters that occur *after* the period in a filename — have changed in Office 2007. For example, newly created Word 2007 files don't use the.doc file extension. Instead, they use .docx (where the "x" stands for XML). As you might guess, the default file extension for new Excel 2007 workbooks is .xlsx. Remember that if you have the display of document file extensions turned off in your Windows settings, you won't see the file extensions when working in Office 2007.

If you open an older file format from a previous version of Office, it displays in *compatibility mode* within Office 2007. This mode means that an older document won't have access to some of the new features in Office 2007 — that is, unless you convert the file to Office 2007 format. However, if you plan to share these files with others who haven't yet upgraded to Office 2007, you shouldn't convert them.

If you want to upgrade a file from a previous version of Office to the latest file format in Office 2007, follow these steps:

1. **Open the older file in the appropriate Office 2007 application.**

2. **Click the Microsoft Office button (the round Windows icon in the upper left corner of the window) to open the File menu.**

3. **Choose Convert.**

   This option displays *only* when you're viewing a file in an older file format.

4. **If you see a dialog box with a message stating that you're about to convert the document to the newest file format, click OK.**

5. **Click the Microsoft Office button and then click Save to save the file in the new Office 2007 format.**

   Or, click Save As and specify a new filename if you want to retain the previous version of the file in the older format.

Accessing Commands via the Keyboard

Some of you may prefer to keep your hands on the keyboard and reach for that mouse only when necessary. Good news — you won't need to change your habits in Office 2007. Remember the old standby keyboard shortcuts, such as Ctrl+C to copy, Ctrl+X to cut, and Ctrl+V to paste? Well, all the shortcuts that start with the Ctrl key remain unchanged and are usable in Office 2007.

However, the keyboard shortcuts that start with the Alt key do have changes. When you press Alt in an Office 2007 application, you'll see *KeyTips* — small letter indicators — displayed onscreen.

Follow these steps to choose commands via the keyboard:

1. **Press and release the Alt key.**

   The KeyTip indicators display next to the tab names at the top of the ribbon and beside the buttons on the Quick Access toolbar. You'll also see an "F" indicator beside the Microsoft Office button (for File menu).

2. **Press the displayed letter indicator for the feature you want.**

   Or press F to access the File menu.

3. **Continue pressing the letter(s) until you choose the command you want.**

   What happens next depends on the chosen command. Either the action takes place, or you see a dialog box or pane.

Zooming and Shrinking the Display

Want to quickly zoom in on your document to get a closer look or zoom out to see the big picture? Zooming in and out is easier than ever in Office 2007.

Locate the Zoom slider in the bottom right corner of the screen. Drag the slider toward the plus sign (to the right) to zoom in, or toward the minus sign (to the left) to zoom out. (Access 2007 doesn't include this feature.) If your mouse has a wheel, you can still use it to zoom the display. Hold down the Ctrl key and scroll the wheel forward to zoom in or scroll the wheel backward to zoom out.

If you want to set a custom zoom, click the zoom percentage to the left of the minus sign in the Zoom slider to display the Zoom dialog box. Then, type a custom zoom percentage in the text box or choose another zoom option. You'll also find a Zoom option on the View tab of the ribbon.

Adding Headers and Footers in Excel

Excel 2007 offers an easier way to add headers and footers to a worksheet. You no longer need to use a dialog box. Just switch to Page Layout view (on the View tab) and click in the Click to Add Header area at the top of the page, or the Click to Add Footer area at the bottom of the page. You can click in the left box for a left-aligned header or footer, the center box for a centered header or footer, or the right box for a — you guessed it — right-aligned header or footer.

After you type text in the header or footer area, you see a Design tab and a Header & Footer Tools tab appear on the ribbon. That's where you'll find additional commands for working with headers and footers. Excel 2007 also includes a new option to apply different headers and footers on odd- and even-numbered pages.

Reviewing Your Document

Don't forget to spell-check your document when you're done working with it. Can't seem to find this feature within the new Office 2007 user interface? That doesn't give you an excuse to omit this important step.

In Word 2007, the Spelling & Grammar command appears in the Proofing group of the Review tab. This location also applies to Excel 2007 and PowerPoint 2007, but the command name is Spelling. In Access 2007, the Spelling command is located in the Records group on the Home tab.

If you need to change how an application corrects your text or access other proofing tools, click the Microsoft Office button and then click the Options button below the File menu (such as Excel Options within Excel 2007). In the Options dialog box that displays, click Proofing in the left pane. Make the desired changes in the right pane and click OK.

Printing and Sending a Document

Before you print or share a document, it's always a good idea to preview the document on-screen to see how it *really* looks. Surprisingly, the ribbon has no Print Preview command. To find this command, click the Microsoft Office button (remember, it's that round icon in the upper left corner of the window). Then, point to the arrow beside the Print command and click Print Preview from the resulting list.

If you need to make adjustments to the document before printing, click the Page Layout tab of the ribbon. Many of the settings you'll need are in the Page Setup group. If you need additional setup options, click the dialog box launcher (the little arrow icon in the lower right corner of the Page Setup group) to display the Page Setup dialog box.

When you're finally ready to print, you can do so by clicking the Print button in the Quick Access toolbar (near the top left corner of the application window). This option immediately prints one copy of the current document to the current printer. If you need to specify other printing options in the Print dialog box, click the Microsoft Office button and then click Print.

In Word 2007, Excel 2007, and PowerPoint 2007, you'll see a Send option on the File menu (click the Microsoft Office button). This is where you find options for e-mailing and faxing documents. Access 2007 includes an Email option on the File menu.

Publishing Document Content

The Publish command on the File menu (remember to click the Microsoft Office button to access this menu) offers even more options for getting your Word 2007, Excel 2007, and PowerPoint 2007 files out there.

Here, you discover options for creating a blog post with document content in Word, sharing and synchronizing documents, and packaging and publishing a PowerPoint presentation, among other things.

Getting Help When You Need It

Where did the Help menu go? You might notice that the ribbon doesn't include a Help tab or command either. You can get help by clicking the blue icon with the question mark in the upper right corner of the application window. The F1 function key still works, too.

Of course, more Help options are available if you're online at the time you access Help. If you're connected to the Internet, you can find more comprehensive (and updated) Help from Office Online.

If you see a command or button on the ribbon and you're not sure what it does, try pointing to the command to see a description. If a keyboard shortcut goes with the command (such as Ctrl+B for Bold), you'll see it displayed, too.

Chapter 12

Ten Ways to Keep Windows from Breaking

*I*f your computer seems to be running reasonably well, stay right here. This chapter gives you ten ways to keep it running that way for the longest time possible.

This chapter is a checklist of sorts, with each section explaining a fairly simple and necessary task to keep Windows running at its best. There's no need to call in a techie because much of this takes place using either Windows' built-in maintenance tools or standard household cleaners. For example, you run Vista's built-in Disk Cleanup program to free up space on a crowded hard disk.

This chapter also helps you fix the annoying and ubiquitous "bad driver" problem by explaining how to put a fresh driver behind the wheel.

Finally, you discover a quick way to clean your mouse — a necessary but oft-overlooked task that keeps the pointer on target. (Feel free to grab the vacuum cleaner and suck all the cookie crumbs out of your keyboard during the same cleaning spree.)

In addition to the checklist this chapter offers, make sure Vista's Windows Update and Windows Defender programs are running on auto-pilot. They both go a long way to keep your computer running safely and securely.

Create a Restore Point

When your computer's ailing, System Restore provides a magical way to go back in time to when your computer was feeling better. System Restore works by taking a daily snapshot of your computer's settings, as well as an automatic snapshot before you install a new computer part (just in case the newcomer causes problems).

The problem is finding that one, magic restore point that makes everything better. Windows Vista simply slaps a date onto its automated System Restore points along with the boring name *System Checkpoint: Scheduled Checkpoint;* it doesn't say, "This restore point is just after installing Berzerkeroids — and everything still ran fine!"

To maximize System Restore's potential, create your *own* restore points with your *own* labels. Here's how to create your own Restore Point on a particularly auspicious day:

1. **Click the Start menu, choose All Programs, select Accessories, choose System Tools, and select System Restore.**

   The System Restore window appears.

2. **Choose Open System Protection and click the Create button.**

   The System Properties window opens to display the System Protection page.

   This same page in Windows XP offers a handy Create a Restore Point option. Vista, by contrast, complicates matters by leading you to a tab on the crowded System Properties window, hoping you'll spot the Create button near the bottom.

   Vista turns on System Restore automatically, but give the window a quick eyeball to make sure that it *stayed* turned on. It's turned on if you spot a checkmark in the top box. That means System Restore is turned on for your C: drive — the first and only hard drive in most people's computers.

Don't bother to turn on System Restore for any other drives you see, should you have any. System Restore saves only files essential to Windows' operating system, which all live out on C:.

3. **When Windows asks you to describe your new restore point, type something that helps you remember why you're making this particular restore point.**

For example, type in Running great, because nothing has crashed for a week! Windows automatically time and date stamps your Restore Point, so don't bother typing the date.

4. **Click the Create button.**

Windows Vista creates a Restore Point with that name.

By creating your own restore points on good days, you'll know immediately which ones to use on bad days.

Back Up Your Computer

Your hard drive will eventually die, unfortunately, and it will take everything with it: Years of digital photos, songs, letters, financial records, scanned items, and anything else you've created or stored on your PC.

That's why it's important to back up your files on a regular basic. That second copy lets you pick up the pieces gracefully when your hard drive suddenly walks off the stage.

Windows Vista's solution, its bundled Backup program, offers a rare combination: It's basic *and* awkward to use. But if you have more time than money, here's how to make Windows Vista's built-in Backup program back up your important files. If you prefer something a little easier to use, ask your computer retailer to recommend a third-party backup program that's both more dependable and easier to use.

Before you can use Windows Vista's Backup program, you need three things:

✔ **A CD burner, DVD burner, or external hard drive:** Windows' free Backup program can write to CDs and DVDs — if you're willing to sit there and feed those discs to your PC. But for dependable, automatic backups, nothing beats an external hard drive. Buy one that simply plugs into your computer's FireWire or USB 2.0 port; Vista recognizes it on the spot.

✔ **An Administrator account:** You must be logged on to the computer with an Administrator account.

✔ **Windows Vista's Backup program:** The Backup program comes free in every version of Windows Vista. Unfortunately, the backup program doesn't run *automatically* in Windows Home Basic — you must remember to run it every evening. (That's one of the reasons that version costs less than the Home Premium and Ultimate versions of Vista.)

When you take care of those three things, follow these steps to make your computer back up your work automatically each month (good), week (better), or night (best):

1. **Open the Vista's Backup and Restore Center.**

   Click Start, choose Control Panel, choose System and Maintenance, and select Back Up and Restore Center.

   You can also launch backup by typing **backup** into the Start menu's Search box.

2. **Choose Set Up Backup.**

   The Backup and Restore Center offers two slightly different ways to back up your PC. But you want to choose File and Folder Backup by clicking its adjacent Set Up Backup button.

   The thoughtful program asks where you want to save the files.

3. **Choose where to save your backup and click Next.**

   Vista lets you save your backup nearly anywhere: CDs, DVDs, USB drives, portable hard drives, or even a drive on a networked computer.

   Although your choice depends on the amount of information you're backing up, the best solution is a *portable hard drive*: A hard drive in a box that plugs into one of your PC's USB or FireWire ports.

A portable hard drive lets you schedule backups to take place *automatically*, every day. The other solutions all require you to sit at your PC, slowly feeding it discs for each backup. That turns your daily backup into an "Oh, I'll just do it tomorrow" thing, unfortunately, that somehow never gets done.

If you can't afford a portable hard drive, then CDs or DVDs are the next best thing.

If you try to save to a networked drive on another PC, Vista asks for an administrator account's username and password on the other PC.

4. **Choose the types of files you want to back up and click Next.**

   Although Windows asks what types of files you want to back up, it's already selected *every* type of file on the list. If you have a very good reason for not backing some of them up, remove the checkmarks next to those files.

   If you don't remove any checkmarks, Vista backs up all the files in every user account on the PC.

   What Vista won't back up, though, are programs. But because you've saved their installation disks, you can simply reinstall them.

   Vista saves every file and folder in each users' User Account folder. To be precise, that's the C:\Users folder, including all the folders inside it.

5. **Choose how often to backup and click the Save Settings and Start Backup button.**

   Choose Daily, Weekly, or Monthly and then choose the day and time for the backup program to kick in. You can choose a time when you'll already be working on your PC, but the backup will slow down your PC.

   For the most convenient backups, choose a Daily backup taking place in the wee hours. If you turn off your PC at night, choose a daytime schedule.

   When you click the Save Settings and Start Backup button, Vista immediately starts its backup — even if one's not scheduled yet. That's because the ever-vigilant Vista wants to make sure it grabs everything right now — before something goes wrong.

Note: Vista Home Basic doesn't offer this option.

6. **Restore a few files to test your backup.**

Now it's time to make sure that everything worked. Repeat the first step, but choose Restore Files. Follow the menus until you can browse the list of backed-up files. Right-click a test file and click the Restore button to make sure that it's copied back to place.

When creating backups, keep the following points in mind:

✔ For your computer to back up automatically each night, you must leave it *turned on* during the scheduled backup time. I leave mine turned on 24 hours a day. (Please turn off your computer's monitor when not in use, though.)

✔ Vista saves your file in a folder named Vista in the location you chose in Step 3. It names the file after the date of the backup. Don't change that file's or folder's location. Vista may not be able to find it again when you choose to restore it.

✔ Every week or so, right-click your backup file, choose Properties, and check the file's Modified date. If you're backing up at 4 a.m., the backup file's Modified date is the current date. If the date's wrong, fire up the Backup program and walk through these steps to figure out the problem.

✔ After making its first backup, Vista starts backing up only the files that have changed since your last backup. Don't be surprised if subsequent backups are faster or don't require as many CDs or DVDs. Eventually, Vista tells you it's time for another complete backup, which takes longer.

Finding Technical Information about Your Computer

 If you ever need to look under Windows Vista's hood, heaven forbid, open the Control Panel's System and Maintenance section and choose System. The System window offers an easily digestible technical briefing about your PC's viscera:

- ✔ **Windows Version:** Vista comes in way-too-many versions to remember. To jog your memory, Vista lists the version that's running on your PC.

- ✔ **System:** Here, Vista rates your PC's strength — its *System Performance Rating* — on a scale of 1 (frail) to 5 (robust). Your PC's type of *CPU* (Central Processing Unit) also appears here, as well as its amount of memory.

- ✔ **Computer Name and Workgroup:** This tab identifies your computer's name, as well as the network it's joined (if it's part of a network, that is).

- ✔ **Windows Activation:** To keep people from buying one copy of Windows Vista and installing it on several PCs, Microsoft requires Windows Vista to be *activated*, a process that chains it to a single PC.

The pane along the left also lists some more advanced Tasks you may find handy during those panic-stricken times when something's going wrong with your PC. Here's the rundown:

- ✔ **Device Manager:** This lists all the parts inside your computer, but not in a friendly manner. Parts with exclamation points next to them aren't happy. Double-click them and choose Troubleshoot to diagnose their problem.

- ✔ **Remote Settings:** Rarely used, this complicated setup lets other people control your PC through the Internet, hopefully to fix things. If you can find one of these helpful people, let them walk you through this procedure over the phone, or through an instant messaging program.

- ✔ **System Protection:** This lets you create Restore Points (described in this chapter's first section), as well as to let a Restore Point take your PC back to another point in time — hopefully when it was in a better mood.

- ✔ **Advanced System Settings:** Professional techies spend lots of time in here. Everybody else ignores it.

Most of the stuff listed in the Vista's System area is fairly complicated, so don't mess with it unless you're sure of what you're doing or a technical support person tells you to change a specific setting.

Rearrange Items on Your Hard Disk to Make Programs Run Faster

When writing information to your hard disk, Windows isn't the most careful shelf stocker. It often breaks files into pieces, stuffing them into different nooks and crannies. When rummaging around for all the parts, Windows subsequently takes longer to retrieve the files.

To fix the problem, Vista automatically sets aside some time each week to restock its shelves, manually reassembling all the file's many pieces into one easy-to-grab chunk.

To make sure that Vista's on the job, open the Control Panel and select System and Maintenance. In the Administrative Tools section along the bottom, select Defragment Your Hard Drive.

When the Disk Defragmenter window appears, make sure that a checkmark appears next to Run Automatically (Recommended). If the scheduled time is inconvenient — perhaps you turn off your PC at night — feel free to reschedule the defragmenting for a different time, perhaps when you know your PC is turned on. (Disk Defragmenter shares the same scheduler as Vista's Backup scheduler.)

The Disk Defragmenter will do its job in the background as you work, if need be. Sometimes it finishes in a few minutes, other times it works through the evening. When it's finished, your computer opens and closes files more quickly.

Free Up Space on Your Hard Disk

Vista grabs more space on your hard drive than any other version of Windows. If programs begin whining about running out of room on your hard disk, this solution grants you a short reprieve:

1. **Choose Start, select Control Panel, choose System and Maintenance, and select Free Up Disk Space in the Administrative Tools category.**

   The Disk Cleanup Options box appears.

2. **Choose whether to clean up only *your* files or *all* of the files on the computer.**

   Cleaning up *all* the files on the computer frees up more space, but that also means you'll be emptying the Recycle Bin of everybody who uses the PC. Because some people may not want their trash emptied, Vista asks for an Administrator password.

   If you don't hold an Administrator account, choose My Files Only. But if you're an administrator and want to empty every account's Recycle Bin, choose All Files on This Computer.

   Vista presents the Disk Cleanup window.

   If your PC has more than two hard drives, Vista asks you to choose which hard drive to clean. Choose your C: drive, as that's the drive that needs cleaning the most.

3. **Click Delete Files when Windows Vista asks whether you're sure.**

   Windows Vista then proceeds to empty your Recycle Bin, destroy leftovers from old Web sites, and remove other hard disk clutter.

For a shortcut to Disk Cleanup, click the Start menu and type **disk cleanup** in the Search box.

Empower Your Power Button

Normally, a press of a PC's power button turns off your PC, whether Vista's ready or not. That's why you should always turn off Vista with its *own* Off button, found by clicking the Start menu, clicking the little arrow by the lock icon, and choosing Shut Down. That gives Vista time to prepare for the event.

To avoid jolting Vista with an unexpected shutdown, consider reprogramming your laptop or PC's power button so that it doesn't turn off your PC at all. Instead, it sends it to the type of slumber you desire: Sleep or Hibernate.

To change your power button's mission, open the Control Panel, choose System and Maintenance, and select Power Options. The Power Options window appears.

From the left side panel, click Choose What the Power Button Does. There, you can tell your power button to either Sleep, Hibernate, or Shut Down your PC.

For extra security, click Require a Password so that anybody waking up your PC will need your password to see your information.

 For quick access to this area, type **power options** into the Start menu's Search box. Laptop owners will see an additional option letting them change how their laptop reacts when they close its lid.

Set Up Your Devices That Don't Work

Windows comes with an arsenal of *drivers* — software that lets Windows communicate with the gadgets you plug into your PC. Normally, Vista automatically recognizes your new part, and it works. Other times, Vista heads to the Internet and fetches some instructions before finishing the job.

But occasionally, you'll install something that's either too new for Windows Vista to know about or too old for it to remember. Or perhaps something attached to your PC no longer works right, and Vista's Welcome Center grumbles about needing a "new driver."

In these cases, it's up to you to track down and install a Windows Vista driver for that part. The best drivers come with an installation program that automatically places the software in the right place. The worst drivers leave all the grunt work up to you.

If Windows Vista doesn't automatically recognize and install your newly attached piece of hardware — even after you restart your PC — follow these steps to locate and install a new driver:

1. **Visit the part manufacturer's Web site and download the latest Windows Vista driver.**

   You often find the manufacturer's Web site stamped somewhere on the part's box. If you can't find it, try searching for the part manufacturer's name on Google (www.google.com) and locate its Web site.

   Look in the Web site's Support or Customer Service area. There, you usually need to enter your part, its model number, and your computer's operating system (Windows Vista) before the Web site coughs up the driver.

   No Windows Vista driver listed? Try downloading a Windows 2000 driver instead because they sometimes work just as well. (Be sure to scan *any* downloaded file with a virus checker.)

2. **Run the driver's installation program.**

   Sometimes clicking your downloaded file makes its installation program jump into action, installing the driver for you. If so, you're through. If not, head to Step 3.

    If the downloaded file has a little zipper on the icon, right-click it and choose Extract All to *unzip* its contents into a new folder. (Vista names that new folder after the file you've unzipped, making it easy to relocate.)

3. **Open the Control Panel, choose Hardware and Sound, and then select Device Manager.**

   The Device Manager appears, listing an inventory of every part inside or attached to your computer.

4. **Click anywhere inside the Device Manager, click Action, and then choose Add Legacy Hardware.**

   The Add Hardware Wizard guides you through the steps of installing your new hardware and, if necessary, installing your new driver.

Here are a few tips to keep in mind:

- ✔ Keep your drivers up-to-date. Even the ones packaged with newly bought parts are usually old. Visit the manufacturer's Web site and download the latest driver.

Chances are, it fixes problems earlier users had with the first set of drivers.

✔ Problems with the new driver? Open the Control Panel, choose System and Maintenance, and select Device Manager. Then double-click your part's name — *Keyboards,* for example — on the window's left side. Vista reveals the make and model of your part. Double-click the part's name and click the Driver tab on the Properties box. Breathe steadily. Finally, click the Roll Back Driver button. Windows Vista ditches the newly installed driver and returns to the previous driver.

Clean Your Mouse

If your mouse pointer jumps around on-screen or doesn't move at all, your mouse is probably clogged with desktop gunk. Follow these steps to degunkify it:

1. **Turn the mouse upside down and clean off any dirt stuck to the bottom.**

   Your mouse must lie flat on its pad to work correctly.

2. **Inspect the bottom of your mouse.**

   If your mouse has a little ball on the bottom, proceed to Step 3.

   If your mouse has a little light on the bottom, proceed to Step 4.

3. **Cleaning a mouse with a ball:**

   Twist off the mouse's little round cover and remove the ball. Wipe off any crud from the ball and blow dust out of the hole. A little compressed air blower, sold at office and computer stores, works well here. (It also blows off the dust layers clogging your computer's air vents.)

   Pull out any stray hairs, dust, and roller goo. A cotton swab moistened with some alcohol cleans the most persistent goo from the little rollers. (The rollers should be smooth and shiny.) Dirty rollers cause the most mouse problems.

Replace the cleaned ball into the cleaned hole and reinsert the clean little round cover.

4. Cleaning an optical mouse:

An optical mouse replaces the old-fashioned rubber ball with a tiny laser. With no moving parts, optical mice rarely need cleaning. But if yours is acting up, remove any stray hairs clinging to the bottom around the light.

Also, make sure that the mouse rests on a textured surface that's not shiny. If your desktop is glass or shiny (polished wood grain, for example), put your optical mouse on a mouse pad for best traction.

If your newly cleaned mouse still has problems, it may be time for a new one. But before shelling out the cash, check these things:

- ✔ Wireless mice go through batteries fairly quickly. If your mouse doesn't have a connecting cord, it's wireless. Check its battery and make sure that it's within range of its receiving unit. (The receiving unit plugs into your PC, perhaps in the back.)

- ✔ Check your mouse's settings: Choose Start, open the Control Panel and choose Mouse in the Hardware and Sound category. Look through the settings to see whether something's obviously wrong.

Clean Your Monitor

Don't spray glass cleaner directly onto your monitor because it drips down into the monitor's guts, frightening the circuits. Instead, spray the glass cleaner onto a soft rag and wipe the screen. Don't use paper because it can scratch the glass.

For cleaning flat panel monitors, use a soft, lint-free cloth, and a mix of half water and half vinegar. Feel free to clean your monitor's front panels, too, if you're feeling especially hygienic.

Clean Your Keyboard

Keyboards are usually too wide to shake over a wastebasket. The best way to clean them is to shut down Windows, turn off your computer, and unplug the keyboard from the computer. (If your keyboard has a rectangular plug that pushes into a USB port, there's no need to turn off your PC.)

Take the keyboard outdoors and shake it vigorously to remove the debris. If the keyboard's grimy, spray some household cleaning solution onto a rag and wipe off any goo from around the keyboard's edges and its keycaps.

Plug it back in, turn on your computer, and your computer looks almost new.

Index

Notes

Notes

....

_____

_____

_____

_____

_____

_____

_____

_____

_____

_____

_____

_____

_____

_____

_____

_____

_____

_____

SPORTS, FITNESS, PARENTING, RELIGION & SPIRITUALITY

0-7645-5146-9

0-7645-5418-2

Also available:

- Adoption For Dummies
  0-7645-5488-3
- Basketball For Dummies
  0-7645-5248-1
- The Bible For Dummies
  0-7645-5296-1
- Buddhism For Dummies
  0-7645-5359-3
- Catholicism For Dummies
  0-7645-5391-7
- Hockey For Dummies
  0-7645-5228-7

- Judaism For Dummies
  0-7645-5299-6
- Martial Arts For Dummies
  0-7645-5358-5
- Pilates For Dummies
  0-7645-5397-6
- Religion For Dummies
  0-7645-5264-3
- Teaching Kids to Read
  For Dummies
  0-7645-4043-2
- Weight Training For Dummies
  0-7645-5168-X
- Yoga For Dummies
  0-7645-5117-5

TRAVEL

0-7645-5438-7

0-7645-5453-0

Also available:

- Alaska For Dummies
  0-7645-1761-9
- Arizona For Dummies
  0-7645-6938-4
- Cancún and the Yucatán
  For Dummies
  0-7645-2437-2
- Cruise Vacations For Dummies
  0-7645-6941-4
- Europe For Dummies
  0-7645-5456-5
- Ireland For Dummies
  0-7645-5455-7

- Las Vegas For Dummies
  0-7645-5448-4
- London For Dummies
  0-7645-4277-X
- New York City For Dummies
  0-7645-6945-7
- Paris For Dummies
  0-7645-5494-8
- RV Vacations For Dummies
  0-7645-5443-3
- Walt Disney World & Orlando
  For Dummies
  0-7645-6943-0

GRAPHICS, DESIGN & WEB DEVELOPMENT

0-7645-4345-8

0-7645-5589-8

Also available:

- Adobe Acrobat 6 PDF
  For Dummies
  0-7645-3760-1
- Building a Web Site For Dummies
  0-7645-7144-3
- Dreamweaver MX 2004
  For Dummies
  0-7645-4342-3
- FrontPage 2003 For Dummies
  0-7645-3882-9
- HTML 4 For Dummies
  0-7645-1995-6
- Illustrator cs For Dummies
  0-7645-4084-X

- Macromedia Flash MX 2004
  For Dummies
  0-7645-4358-X
- Photoshop 7 All-in-One Desk
  Reference For Dummies
  0-7645-1667-1
- Photoshop cs Timesaving
  Techniques For Dummies
  0-7645-6782-9
- PHP 5 For Dummies
  0-7645-4166-8
- PowerPoint 2003 For Dummies
  0-7645-3908-6
- QuarkXPress 6 For Dummies
  0-7645-2593-X

NETWORKING, SECURITY, PROGRAMMING & DATABASES

0-7645-6852-3

0-7645-5784-X

Also available:

- A+ Certification For Dummies
  0-7645-4187-0
- Access 2003 All-in-One Desk
  Reference For Dummies
  0-7645-3988-4
- Beginning Programming
  For Dummies
  0-7645-4997-9
- C For Dummies
  0-7645-7068-4
- Firewalls For Dummies
  0-7645-4048-3
- Home Networking For Dummies
  0-7645-42796

- Network Security For Dummies
  0-7645-1679-5
- Networking For Dummies
  0-7645-1677-9
- TCP/IP For Dummies
  0-7645-1760-0
- VBA For Dummies
  0-7645-3989-2
- Wireless All In-One Desk Refere
  For Dummies
  0-7645-7496-5
- Wireless Home Networking
  For Dummies
  0-7645-3910-8